Don't Tell Your Momma You're an Atheist

Don't Tell Your Momma You're an Atheist

Ray J. Egan

Published By OCEAN GROOVE PRESS

Table of Contents

INTRODUCTION

No, I have not told my mother or father I am an atheist. The fact is I am a little embarrassed about it. Not embarrassed the way I might be if I were to be forced to run naked through the streets carrying a cabbage in each hand and, at the same time, singing the alphabet song over and over. More like the feeling that I would be somehow disappointing them in a big way. They are not religious but are traditionally very grounded. My actual belief is benign enough and was arrived at early in life. Such is the real-world position of an atheist; someone who simply believes no God has ever existed. The events, debates and awareness of the subject over the last 10 years or so has simply piqued my interest and allowed me to delve a bit more into why so many people believe in a 'higher power'.

I hope you are reading this book at least partly because you are interested in what I consider to be one of the most controversial and important subjects of the 21st century, namely the 'battle' between Atheists and their God-believing counterparts, over the subject of life's beginnings, evolution and the cosmos, and partly because you have an inclination towards one side or the other and are perhaps interested in having this subject displayed from the perspective of someone who is a non-believer, but neither an intellectual nor a scientist. An 'everyday man', if you will.

In recent years much has been written about atheism and Darwin's Theory of Evolution, and the Internet is filled with interesting and engaging people, each with their own closely held beliefs, and arguing intently for their 'side'. Here, in this book, I intend to show you my atheistic-side-of-things as well as discuss some of the best encounters, interviews and debates I have seen, and give you my opinions on them.

Admittedly, I am in impressive company. Most books on this subject, already on the shelves, have been written by people like Professor Richard Dawkins and others, who provide more 'subject-specific matter' within their writings. One of his most famous books, THE SELFISH GENE was his first, and became a best seller, challenging scientists and others and bringing the study of genes (as they related to evolution) to the general public.

I, on the other hand, wanted to cover more ground and try to touch on a number of areas that would bring in the average reader to the 'whole ball of wax', as it were. All of my facts come from a variety of sources that I cite, and I attempt to interpret them to the best of my ability. Some facts are direct writings from websites and books that again, I have given credit for. You will see a chapter on the history of atheism, and how tough it was (and is) to proclaim one to be an atheist. I have another chapter that talks about the evidence for evolution, and one that is dedicated to an interesting (and disturbing) interview between Professor Dawkins and Wendy Wright, president of the Concerned Women of America.

This book may be interpreted by some to be a challenge to theists, or one that attempts to brush aside the notion of religion and what billions of people around the world believe, in one form or another. Whatever the inference, I DO want to show the results of MY interest and research in these areas, even if only superficially. I hope that this is an interesting easy-read for most of you and that the average person (whether religiously-inclined or not) can appreciate my position, as one who would like to think that reason, evidence, science, and maybe even just a little common-sense can be used (as we do in every other facet of our lives) to come to the conclusion that we are all here by natural 'causation', and nothing more.

Just to be clear, I am wearing the atheistic shoes for this book. I am also by no means a card-carrying atheist (if there IS such a thing). My simple perspective is that I believe their to be no evidence that has crossed my table that would suggest there to be an all-seeing creator (or ANY god)), as I had long ago discovered the Theory of Evolution and have a profound 'faith' (?) in our scientists in the fields of astrophysics, molecular biology, Quantum physics and more, as well as in the advanced DNA techniques and genome projects that are going to reveal (and have revealed) some amazing truths on the connectivity to our distant ancestors. I will include, in this book, a basic discussion on Darwin's theory and some insight as to why so many people from the theistic side have trouble with it. Additionally, to be clear, as well as stating arguments which are 'pro-atheist', I will be analyzing some of the responses and counter-arguments that have been made during some of the more popular debates from the Internet. Some chapters will contain information about the Judeo-Christian bible that is worth delving into, and others will offer some interesting observations on some interviews I have seen. I can also easily admit that most of these arguments that I will be postulating in this book are not exclusively my own. But I agree with them.

Initially, I started writing this book somehow to add my own layman's atheistic viewpoint for the benefit of those religiously-inclined folks who may think that atheists have a sinister agenda or want religion totally banned from the planet, and partly to go over the basic arguments that have been presented by the atheists/evolutionists that have, as far as I can tell, not yet been addressed well nor successfully counter-argued by theists in these debates. Atheism is NOT a religion and that topic will be broached as well. It seems, though, I have learned far more than I thought I would, upon researching for this book. I have seen, through various debates, very learned, intelligent, fervently religious people confidently stake their position solid amongst all who would oppose them (namely atheists and evolutionists). I have also seen how far some are willing to go, EVEN IN THE FACE OF LEGITIMATE CRITICISM and REASONED OPINIONS, holding fast to their belief in an all-knowing, all-caring 'father' god.

I have been tempted a few times to respond as an anti-theist to friends and colleagues who are ardently religious. One recent encounter with an older lady in my area stopped by to see how I was doing after a chemical-in my-left-eye accident. We sat down in my living room, and somehow the subject of my faith came up. She was genuinely surprised at my atheism. If I can remember her exact wording. "I can't believe such a nice guy as you would not believe in god." I left it there, although the temptation to 'get into it' was hard to resist.

If any of you have had the opportunity to view these many debates on the internet featuring people like Professor Richard Dawkins, a skilled biologist, educator, atheist and a proponent of the Darwinian Theory of Evolution by natural selection and Rabbi Shmuley Boteach , who has written 19 books, the most recent one 'The Broken American Male' and is host of his own show on the OPRAH network, then you know how entertaining and informative these confrontations can be. You can also see that there is still a fairly big gap between those that live their lives by religion (in widely-varying degrees) and those that take a more reasoned, evidence-based standpoint on the issues of whether or not a supreme-being exists, and of the theories of the origins of the universe as well as of all life on our planet.

These are some of the most important questions we can ask, as well as being necessary for trying to find out what is true and what is not, and I hope that I have contributed to this topic in some small way.

Chapter One

The Basics

Why are there so many different religions all over the place? That, I recall, was the first question I overheard someone say when I was about 14 years old that got me thinking in a new direction. I admit it was not the thunder-and-lightening epiphany one could get when confronted by a whole new world, a world where perhaps, just perhaps, there was no all-seeing, all-knowing, benevolent super-natural force that created everything around us (Deist), or one who stays with us all, telling us what to do, what to eat (and on what day). One might say an INTRUSIVE god (Theist).

Up to that point I had a fairly non-existent upbringing by way of religion. My mom and dad were from the Church of England. As usual, I would have been considered an 'Anglican baby' and I started Sunday school at around 4 years of age. I don't have too many recollections of that time. I DO recall sitting in a circle with other children and I have vague memories of a book with the 3 wise men, shepherds and the basic stories of Jesus and his family.

Neither of my parents would I consider religious. They are the sweetest people I know and they simply have, what I would consider to be a very common, cultural and traditional view of the church and its goings-on. We used to go to church perhaps once each year for a Christmas celebration, but even then I recall only a few times. Mostly I did not want to go. I'm not too sure if that was because boys-will-be-boys and my desire to hang out and play with my friends overshadowed a trip to an unusual, sermon-filled occasion or not, but I always had a strange, nervous feeling about the whole thing. Without even knowing what a cult was, I intuitively rejected the whole process as if I were to be indoctrinated into something that I was simply not ready for.

As I unconsciously (at first) rejected the concept of a supreme being I began to think a little bit more about it. No, I did not sit around all day pondering the big question, but there were plenty of people around me who would sometimes mention god and/or religion and it struck me that more people believed in this thing than I did. Constantly I would hear the oft-benign phrase 'thank God' uttered by people in everyday conversation, but I realized that, in and of itself, the phrase meant nothing to most of the people saying it; just a figure of speech. I mean, how could ANYONE in good faith THANK god, for example, for saving SOME people from a fiery plane crash when some people died? I never heard, "damn god, he let them die". In later years, I would find that there ARE people who actually take the bible literally!

It was around the age of 15 that I got into talking to my church-going friends and enjoyed the back-and-forth arguments we each had for our side. As one can imagine, it did not take too long for our discussions to wind down to nothing as soon as we could not figure out anything more to say. Truth-be-told, at that time I was having far too much fun learning to play the trombone, setting up a photo studio in my parent's basement (where I would develop the film out of my camera and then the prints themselves) and gazing through my 2-inch refracting telescope at the moon, to really care about the religion stuff. The back-and-forths were fun while they lasted, but were only really a diversion.

The interesting thing is, that for all my desire to write this book, to get my layman's perspective on Atheism and Darwin's' Evolutionary theory and its modern implications out there in a way that I might be able to bridge the gap between the intellectual discussions and the folks who don't really know about them, I had not thought about my atheistic position until 2008. It was really an Internet search that started it all for me. Recently, I was approached by an old friend of mine and he wanted to know how long modern man had been on our planet (not knowing exactly) and I took some time to 'Google' my query.

It was at that time that I encountered an array of interviews; debates and discussions centered around one central thesis. Debates about evolution versus intelligent design permeated the web and I was, indeed, captivated by these folks. The fact that most were scientists and high-level clergy, knowledgeable and intellectual, made their arguments that much more interesting for me. I found myself cheering for 'my side' and wondering why the other side often failed to meet their points head-on.

I do have a few favorites, a small handful of protagonists of the Natural world, and the first one (as you already know) would have to be professor Richard Dawkins. A man of obvious intelligence, he is easy to listen to and seems to have the patience of a saint (lol) when confronted by seemingly obstinate and impenetrable religious apologists. A Biologist, Zoologist, educator, atheist and novelist, he brings all these to his game and delivers his points in an easy-to-get, insightful and sometimes humorous way.

Christopher Hitchens is a man I found out about fairly recently. I immediately was attracted to his swaggering demeanor; his ability to say what he means and his promises to be the 'extremist' in the room. His points, by the way, are nothing short of erudite and well thought out. He is a prolific author and an anti-theist. He claims not to be a scientist but has obviously versed himself in the up-to-date happenings in the scientific world. Both of these men are constantly in the public eye. One can see them on book tours, debating theologians and theists on television and radio interviews.

There are many pro-religious intellectuals on the debating tour as well. Most I find engaging and most seem to believe what they believe and are eloquent in their delivery. There have been a few one-on-one debates and discussions with Richard Dawkins, however, in which I actually had to turn the computer off! One comes to mind. A stand-up talk with Wendy Wright of the Concerned Women of America was just too painful to watch. I DID manage to see all 7 clips from the Internet, however, and as intelligent as she seems, I was amazed at her relative ignorance and blatant dismissal of simple facts. She was, after all, talking to a world-renowned biologist. I mean.. What was she thinking?? More on that later.

Atheists do come in all shapes and sizes, personal histories and beliefs that may have included a theist beginning, but, nonetheless, ended up with a more reasoned and evidence-based opinion on religion. Some of the most renowned atheists today have admitted to some levels of religious indoctrination, but somewhere along the way their opinions changed. Why? In my research, I have found that most 'came to their senses' around their teenage years, realizing that that were many existing religions and reasoning that these totally different doctrines cannot all be right and true, so probably none of them were. For the record (unless I neglect to mention it again), atheism is NOT a religion. With the exception of a 'fringe' element (of which I am not aware) that exists in ANY area of discussion, there are no rituals, no meeting places, unless they all want to get together and share ideas or listen to one of the main proponents while they are on tour, no doctrine that they follow. Theists will argue that there are many different types of atheists but that is simply another attempt to cloud the issue. That's one of the reasons I wrote this book. Let's stick to some of the main issues. VOLUMES of books could be written, and have been, about all the combinations and permutations of theories on the histories of each religion and belief and, well, the idea is to get at the truth through some kind of evidence and verified fact. So let's try to do that.

Unlike the change-of-thought of a 'born-again' Christian, or similar 'theistic shift', whereby the person in question has some sort of unexplained personal connection or experience with the divine being, the 'atheist-to-be' ultimately decides for him or herself BASED ON THE FACTS AND EVIDENCE (somewhat on their study and/or enquiry into evolutionary theory) that evolution presents a much more logical and reason-based theory of the beginnings of man than the deistic one purported by religion. It is also important, here, to mention the 'mild-indoctrination' that takes place throughout the world where religion is concerned. Admittedly, the majority of religious people takes part in sparse religious services and rarely thinks about it in the course of a day. There is, however, a cultural, traditional feeling that one needs to place one's children in the group to which the parents subscribe. That is, if the parents are Christian then they have a 'Christian baby'. This is something I do not agree with and is one of the negative influences religion has in our society.

I came to my atheistic beliefs as an adult (even though I new 'something was up' at the age of 12) and did not really feel (as I mentioned in the introduction) that I was forced into any belief (harmless Sunday school for a year?) And that I came upon my beliefs as a mature adult, knowing as many facts as I felt I needed to in order to 'take a stand', one way or the other. This all might seem harmless, but it is just one more reason that people seem to want to be different from others, yet blame others for BEING different (as in many wars throughout history that have been caused, at least in part, by these differences). Let your offspring think for themselves as adults. Please don't force them to have one 'god-belief' system, as there are many major religions on this planet. ALL of them can't be the real truth, so either they all have to be...... Or NONE of them are.

We will delve more into an explanation of Darwin's theory and the recent modern advancements that improve on it in a later chapter. It is interesting to note however that a large number of scientists and intellectuals today (even a healthy number of bishops, cardinals and priests) believe in evolution. I know what you are thinking. How can that be? The simple answer is that they are willing to agree with the science that has shown them incontrovertible evidence of the evolutionary 'family tree', and that we are all inter-connected in one way or another. If you purport to be objective in your observations and make an attempt to understand, or at the very least look at the mountain of evidence for evolution by natural selection, then, I contend, you cannot come to any other conclusion. As far as this belief permeates the theistic side, to any degree, it does so without denigrating their individual belief in a super-natural creator. Evolution simply is stated as being the 'instrument' of god's design. I personally don't ascribe to this, nor do I think the logic is sound, however if it works for some people, then so be it.

The debate between creationists/intelligent design proponents and natural-world protagonists has become quite complicated. It is reasonably stated that the actual argument is all about god, and whether all we see, touch, taste and smell can exist WITHOUT his being real. Essentially that IS my position. I agree with that statement. But it is not as simple as you might think.

Some religious theories I have come across say that certain mysteries of our universe cannot POSSIBLY happen in a purposeless universe without any underlying super-intelligence. They are saying that the universe consists of more than 95% dark matter and forms of energy that we cannot see, nor detect, and that shows an intelligent designer at work. Is it, then, that we have to wait 1,000 years before scientists can actually measure and quantify this 95% before the creationist side caves and pulls out the white flag of surrender?

Other points of contention are the complex theories of how the universe began. Was it always there or was there an actual start to it all? More research showed me a quote from the famous ancient philosopher, Aristotle, who wrote, "*It is impossible that movement should ever come into being or cease to be, for it must always have existed. Nor can time come into being or cease to be.*" As amazing as this guy was, this scares the theistic side such that modern religious-oriented groups have seemed to put aside his notion, and are more concentrating their efforts to delve more into the 'universe had a beginning' theory and therefore, a creator. You will see, later on in this book, that theists try to take apart the notion that the universe had always existed. They NEED this to be the case if their 'uncaused cause' (God) has anything to do with it! They often point to the work created by Albert Einstein and his general relativity theory of 1916, his conclusions that showed the universe was actually expanding. Further discoveries by people such as astronomer Edwin Hubble showed a 'red-shift' in the movements of the galaxies. The further a galaxy is away from us, the more red light from the spectrum is sent our way, showing its movement away from us. This expanding-thing is really getting all the pro-intelligent design folks in a tizzy. These and more will be touched on in later chapters.

It's hard to believe that these concepts are being used as positive points for the theistic side. That the universe had a beginning means an intelligent designer of some sort. Are they saying that the massive explosion sending these galaxies far, far into the void and 'red-shifting' away from us was due to a purposeful setting off of this explosion to create what we see as our universe today? Why would a designer so powerful have to do all that? That would have been billions of years ago. If we, humans on earth, were his ultimate creation, would there not be a more simple explanation for our existence and perhaps a shortcut as well? (Occam's razor comes to mind). It almost sounds like a magician pulling a rabbit out of a hat but, before doing so, reads the history of the rabbit and the origins of hats and why he became a magician and so on. PULL THE DARN BUNNY OUT OF THE HAT, for Pete's sake!

Another way that theologians and theists have used scientific facts to try help their side along is to use the concept of the 2nd law of thermodynamics, otherwise known as the Second law of First Importance (it supposedly implicates the start of the universe by a designer), because believers say it is essential for their arguments. Don't worry, it is not as complicated as it seems. I came upon this definition. "*Everything continually moves from a state of order to disorder and that heat and energy dissipate over time.*" The religious theorize that if the universe was always there, as some evolutionists claim, that a universe that existed way before our comprehension would be a lifeless one, where all the stars and planets would be nothing but dust. Additionally they conclude that because we see a bright sky full of living stars and our own sun spewing hot molten fire then there must be a creator that made it all happen. There are many more so-called 'scientific' claims that theologians use in stating their case for a designer, but we will save those for a bit further along in our discussion.

You can see how potentially complicated this debate can be. Sometimes I feel like calling it a day and saying, "*Look, the bible is written by man. It tells you of the god you all believe in and it has been passed down from 2,000 years ago and it has entrenched itself in our society so you believe it and try to justify it with scientific fact.*"

In fact, the science only complicates their position. Since neither side can PROVE the existence of god, sane, rational-thinking humans CAN come to the conclusion that reason is the best tool we can use and science should not be used to try to justify the existence of a supreme-being that is only in the mind of the believer.

It is a fact that you can FEEL science. You can TOUCH science. Science is palpable whereas blind faith is not. I would have thought that, since the inception of Christianity, that if the world had as much faith in the human spirit as it has had for the deities of times past then perhaps man would be further along by now. Although we still would have fought wars for some reason (territory, trade routes, etc.) we would be a world of free and critical thinkers. Laws would have developed in large communities based on our innate ability to see that solidarity amongst us is paramount for success and happiness. We DO have a natural desire to do well towards others. Our laws would have reflected that. We would not have needed a tablet of stone telling us 'thou shalt not kill'. We do not need an objective source of good behavior to mimic. Societies would soon weed out the bad guys and have some way of dealing with them.

One of my favorite quotes in researching this book comes from a fellow Canadian, Steven Pinker, whose work in evolutionary psychology is well known. The quote refers to how possible it is for our moral sense and instinct to be an evolved deal. Here it is:

"Two features of reality point any rational, self-preserving social agent in a moral direction. And they could provide a benchmark for determining when the judgments of our moral sense are aligned with morality itself... One is the prevalence of nonzero-sum games. In many arenas of life, two parties are objectively better off if they both act in a non-selfish way than if each of them acts selfishly... The other external support for morality is a feature of rationality itself: that it cannot depend on the egocentric vantage point of the reasoner"... Also, have you ever heard of "do unto others as you would have them do unto you"? That phrase is not from any known religious scriptures either, as some might think, although similar sentiments can be found all over the place. Just a thought.

There is also an idea, although not-too-often talked about, that the whole reason people are so vocal about their religious beliefs is 'safety-in-numbers'. If they were in the distinct minority do you think they would stand up and boldly declare their allegiance to an all-powerful creator? They would be carted off to the 'looney-bins'. It would be a feather in the cap of every evolutionist, debating a theist, if the latter were to admit that they have their beliefs because they have been told about them; because they read about God's existence from the bible, a man-made book; because they feel that 2,000 years of their ever-lasting faith can't be wrong. As if the passage of time makes god's existence any truer? If those folks were simply to be honest with us, as to why they are so adamant in asserting their position then we could all go home! True, the actual beginnings of the universe would not be agreed upon in that case (odds are it will never be ANYWAY), but at least we would be farther ahead and could come together for some real serious scientific discovery. Stop stymieing the process people! Science and reason are the best things we have to arrive at the truth.

I keep coming back to this, but another idea put forth by seemingly desperate theists is the notion that Atheism is a religion. Atheism has some form of dark doctrine that threatens the very core of religious thought. Imagine! I suppose that means, by very definition, that evolutionary thinking is a religion too! I again submit that most, shall we call them 'mild atheists', simply believe there is no god.. uh-uh.. No god anywhere. That's it. How is that assertion by the theists going to help their cause?

So what they are saying is that if I don't believe in God then I am involved in a sort of religion? I can tell you MANY things I don't believe in and don't do. How does that make me a member of a nonexistent group? *That's almost like saying not going sailing is a sport*! Show me a written doctrine that all atheists must follow. Show me a cell-phone video of dark and mystifying pagan ceremonies taking place. NOT GOING TO HAPPEN!

A mere CHILD can say god exists. They are told god exists and are told about the cute stories and allowed to read the bible and have it explained to them (I wonder just how many interpretations there are of the bible out there anyway??). They grow up without giving too much thought to the issue. They keep going to church (hopefully not the fundamentalist one though) and lead a normal, albeit benign life (for the purposes of the debate issue) and are not a threat to anyone. The reality of extreme forms of

18

indoctrination, however, does exist. There are also a large number of people, in the United States again, as an example, which are from the fundamentalist and evangelical branch of the Christian faith. Not to tar everybody with the same brush, but a lot of Fundamentalist Christians believe in the literal meaning of the bible! Well, no need to conjure up what THAT might lead to with certain people in that organization. We may come back to these folks later.

This chapter would not be complete if I did not mention the bad things that have happened in our world's history, relevant to religious belief. Perhaps I won't go over them just yet, as we are all here now, despite the terrible deeds, wars, torture and subjugation of our ancestors in the name of religion. It IS our history though, sorry to say. Mention any point in history over the last 2,000 years and I guarantee that religion will be mentioned, usually in a not-too-positive way. Of course we'd rather draw on our past accomplishments, usually of a scientific nature, and we are at the stage we are now. It is fair to say that in the last 150 years we have advanced on an incredible scale. That there is a natural progression towards violence from some devout religious indoctrination and there is clearly none from an atheistic viewpoint will be mentioned a bit further along. I may have to point out here that those supporting religion would argue that most of the scientific discoveries of the past 2,000 years (at least up to the 18th century) have been because of religion. As true as that is it has to be mentioned that of course, when you have the power-and-money position in society, you can afford to hire the best for your purposes. Only in the last 150 years have we finally broken free of religion's grasp and moved ahead exponentially in discovery, technology and critical-thinking.

Looking back for a minute, it is hard to know if pre-16th century science was ham-stringed by religious beliefs or not. One could argue that science of the pre-scientific revolution of the 16th-17th centuries was all about understanding god better, albeit because there was nothing much else going on. It was only due to the non-religious interference, and 'free-thinking' abilities, of people like Sir Isaac Newton and Galileo that helped move scientific discoveries along. OH WAIT!!! Galileo was thrown in jail for writing a scientific book saying that the earth orbited the sun (what a concept!) that was squarely against the beliefs of the church at that time. Oh well people, I tried.

For the record, I would like to point out a fact that I think not too many people think about. The bible (in this case the Judeo-Christian one) was written in Bronze-Age Middle East. It can arguably be stated that the book was our first serious (?) attempt at scientific concepts, our first foray into meta-physics and philosophy, and of a unification of some sort of education. This was our FIRST ATTEMPT. Often times these first attempts are not the best. The thing about that is that the religious-minded still use the same book to live their lives by.

GOD only knows why they do this.

CHAPTER TWO

Why do we bother?

"Attention one-and-all. Stay glued to your seats as we will be having the brightest minds of our generation compete in a knock-down, dragged-out, no-holds-barred, battle-to-the-death".... Well, enough of that. Sometimes after you have watched the intellectuals go at the same topic time and time again in debates, it almost seems like you ARE at the state fair, waiting for the ultimate victorious contestant to walk to front-and-center and take their deserving bows, except that in these important-issue debates one does not get that satisfaction. The real enjoyment comes from listening to folks who really KNOW about this stuff (the topic and, I presume, debating in general) and it is left up to you to select a winner.

Ultimately that selection will be chosen by the side you were on when you walked in the room, or turned on your computer. There have been few, if any, debates in my memory that have left me with a sense of awe in the outcome. 99 times out of 100 (at least with the 2 folks I mentioned in the previous Chapters), I have said in my head. "Of course," at the obvious victory of my side. I have stood by my representatives for the evolution-and-no-creator side of things and have learned a lot by them. They very rarely disappoint. Although it is untrue to say you cannot argue against a reasoned position, unless you are prepared to do so it can be a very rocky road indeed. As I believe the onus of proof should mainly be on the theistic side, they always need to make sure that they have their 'evolutionary-formed' ducks in a row.

I am not here to parrot the proceedings of any particular debate;

rather I want to give my own layman's interpretation of what atheists and their antagonists are saying so we can benefit from the analysis. I think it is fair to say that, since the majority of us are NOT scientists nor are we theologians we should have the right to examine, in our own way, what it is that is being stated in these debates. I am not suggesting for a second that what they are saying is not self-evident (at least from the atheist side), and that most of us DO understand most of what they are saying. It's just always nice to get another point of view. Mine here, as it stands. In another way, if you read any scientific journal and read of the combination and permutations of fringe ideas and complexities of thought relating to our main topic here, you would be amazed. I can't even claim to understand a lot. Talk of String theories and multi-verses, the CHAOS theory and the philosophical perspective of metaphysical cosmology... ARE YOU KIDDING ME? Most seem to bring us away from the basic issues and turn the tables so other scientists can ONLY do the real arguments. Lets try to stick with the basics. Fortunately for me, these debates rarely go into Quantum or Complex System theory or.... My head hurts.

Why waste our time debating theists? After all, I think sometimes the results might not be worth all that effort. As an intellectual exercise I can clearly see its benefits, as one is prodded to come up with some pretty convincing arguments from both sides. In truth, I think that most atheists would rather chat amongst themselves rather than jumping all over theists, trying to wrench answers from them that will, ultimately, never satisfy.

I also find it telling that we, as atheists, need no support group or other stimuli to remind us where we stand. No, we don't need that. Religion, on the other hand cannot survive without that. Mass rally's, regular attendance at church, all to assure that the religion goes on as before. It is to our credit that atheists need no such bolstering of our position. We can, under no strain what so ever, retain our reasoned opinions without threat of damnation. No guilt here, ladies and gentlemen.

As the theistic camp (in my opinion) has the lion's share of the burden of proof however, it forces them to delve into areas that MAY provide ideas as to the POSSIBILITY of God's existence (from philosophical and meta-physical points of view) but hardly solid PROOFS that a god exists, or indeed, ever existed.

Make no mistake, the atheist side can't be uncaring or dismissive in their opponent's position, nor can they be seen as being the slightest bit not skeptical, as if there is anything an atheist hopes to do in debates such as these is to PROMOTE skepticism.

There is a fair amount of consternation over why atheists bother to debate theists at all. Some say it is because they have an agenda and are trying to convert theists to their way of thinking. I disagree on the grounds that one of the main reasons atheists have entered into these confrontations (as anti-theists) is to decry the proselytizing and attempts from the theist camp to convert atheists to some form of Christianity.

As the majority of the world is religious, the words 'atheist' or 'anti-theism' have many negative connotations associated with them. This is another reason why atheists are only too happy to let people know what it is to be an atheist.

I still find it rather interesting that people get offended by religious criticism. Ultimately, they claim that it is a personal thing and that the personal-things-line should not be crossed. They only THINK it's personal because of the 2,000 year entrenchment of their particular religion. That, plus the fact that most people in their community practice that religion. There's the old 'safety-in-numbers' deal again. Let's face it. You worship one god (because you were told to by your family and community) and that's it. By the time you were 18 I would have hoped that you could have had a more objective viewpoint about your religion, but that usually is not the case.

I am not sure what the percentage is in each religious community, but I bet there are folks who don't feel like continuing with the rituals, but have to in order to save face. After all, who wants the elders of your church knocking on your front door wondering why it is you no longer show up for mass of a Sunday?

One interesting deal is the difference between being an ATHEIST or an ANTI-THEIST. Most non-believers in the world would probably fit into the atheist category, as they are simply indifferent to any proposed gods. They could care less. One might say atheism is the milder form of non god-believing people. It is the anti-theists that are openly opposed to anything theistic. No, I'm not saying that they are fundamentalists. I laugh when I read that back to myself, as I can hear the collective ears of hundred's of thousands of theists ears pricking up in interest. No, being an anti-theist simply means that they are the ones who are actively opposing theism instead of keeping it to themselves. An anti-theist would readily admit god's existence if there were incontrovertible evidence to support such a claim.

I believe it is true that more atheists are becoming anti-theistic in approach these days, as more and more theologians are coming out of the woodwork trying to ram their philosophy down our throats. Consequently, more and more atheists have to come out as anti-theists perhaps and defend their position, as well as dispelling myths about what it is to be an atheist.

To be fair, an anti-theistic person goes perhaps a bit further than your garden-variety atheist. The anti-theist realizes that religion (theism) is harmful to society and that it needs to be stopped. Of course, the anti-theist does not use violence to promote these positions. He/she uses critical-thinking, reason, a bit of common-sense, history and a little bit of correct logic to show how religion has harmed our society more than it has helped, and usually does this in debate forums, on television and radio.

I will mention in this book that if there were a supernatural omnipotent being then this would be a far different world in which we presently reside. As a resident of the United States, I appreciate the personal freedoms that I have and would not exchange them for anything. The thought of being controlled by something like that would be too much to take. This, more than any single point, bothers me the most. I fail to see how so many people have been fooled by the organized religions of this world, especially in these modern times. The only bright point I see is that atheism is growing, quite rapidly at least, in other parts of this planet. Europe is far ahead of us in the denial of god's existence. Sadly, the United States seems to still be haunted by the stigma of not believing something religious. True, there are many immigrants of many differing religions, but it all comes down to the same thing, blind faith in a man-made god.

Actually, the statistics look pretty favorable for an 'about-face' of religious affiliation amongst those in the U.S.A. Even though it might be slow in coming, the latest shows that (according to the Pew forum on Religion and Public Life) "*More than one-quarter of American adults (28%) have left the faith in which they were raised in favor of another religion - or no religion at all.*" The study continues with the conclusion that "*If change in affiliation from one type of Protestantism to another is included, 44% of adults have either switched religious affiliation, moved from being unaffiliated with any religion to being affiliated with a particular faith, or dropped any connection to a specific religious tradition altogether.*" Included in this study of interviews with over 35,000 adults it was also shown that "around 16.1 percent of people are firmly in the atheist category." I am not going to muddy these statistics by talking about the 'agnostic-atheist' or the 'agnostic-theist'. At least these facts show a slight awakening to a reality that allows one to think for themselves, rather than believing everything that is told to you.

Parent's, let's continue this trend and not make your child a ward of the religion in which you happen to subscribe. Let them know about all religions and why people believe in them. I think that once they adopt this objective position they will be far better prepared and able to move forward in our amazing world.

CHAPTER Three

The Big Debate

Just what is all the fuss about? Well, I suppose that depends on whom you talk to. Some people say the real question is whether god exists or not. Other folks will say that it is an argument about fundamentalism (with its inherent dangers) and that both sides accuse each other of being just that. Even more state that it is about having creationism and the (so-called) idea of 'intelligent design' being allowed back into the classroom.

For me, I have already stated my own personal beliefs. This is NOT a complicated issue for me. No god exists and the world can do just fine WITHOUT my believing that one DOES exist. The earth will continue to rotate on it's own axis; will continue to rotate in an ellipse around the sun each year. We will continue to love family and friends, flowers will bloom in the spring and the future results of global-warming, good OR bad, will happen without my belief in a super-natural being.

For the benefit of those that have not seen the debates, nor had an inclination to read lots of books on the subject, perhaps I can shed some light on at least some of the more major topics being debated between theists and atheists today. Another chapter or two will be devoted to actual claims by theists and the reasonable rebuttals of those positions.

A key argument from the theistic side was that atheists commonly did not understand the commitment one makes regarding being close to God, etc. It was felt that atheists generally dismiss that as just another one of religion's foibles. Again the atheistic viewpoint deals with the argument directly and simply states that the great majority of non-religious people USED TO BE, and have become, non-religious because they've given up the commitment that they were led into as children, taught in school, taught by their community, church, mosque, temple, etc. Sometimes, even, they have given it up with varying degrees of discomfort and pain, but they understand very well what is involved and what the story is that their opponents, in the discussion, are committed to.

We all know that virtually every religion in the world has their holy book, or 'original manuscript' of the covenants, rules, stories, and parables that combine to form the basis FOR that religion. "*In Judaism you have the TORAH and Hinduism has the BHAVAGA GITA. Islam has the QUR'AN, the Baha'i faith has the KITAB-I-IQAN and Christianity has the NEW TESTAMENT*". Atheists have been accused of having a doctrine, some common base to which all anti-theists subscribe.

"*There is no holy book of atheism and never COULD be,*" states Professor Richard Dawkins in a recent debate. "*Atheism is not a belief system, there is only 'publically-verified' evidence. This goes against the very definition of fundamentalism's strict adherence to a holy book, and rather states that atheism 'contains a commitment to change, as soon as new evidence comes in.*"

Along with the accusations of Atheism being Fundamentalist, there is also the misconception that we know all there is to know, that we know 'the truth'. In fact, any intelligent atheist runs pretty much along the same lines as the thought processes of scientists. That is to say that we glory in what we yet DON'T know. We are not bored with the past (as theists would accuse us, relating to our relative disinterest in the history of the bible, for instance) but rather we are excited by what it leads on to. What we DON'T know. It can be, again, compared to the scientific arena where the gaps in our knowledge (the fossil record, as we have already talked about, for example) are the source of derision from the theistic side. They maintain that, because of large gaps in our evidence or knowledge that no more questions have to be asked, the answer is that 'god did it'. On the contrary, scientists and atheists alike take pride in the fact that they are ready to 'roll up their sleeves and get down to working out things', attempting to FILL IN those gaps. "*Any attempt to de-rail atheistic, rational, critical thought by claiming a holy book written by ancient, desert nomads is the answer, is foolish indeed.*" Dawkins concludes, "*Science may not know what happened before the 'Big Bang', science may not know yet how life began, but if SCIENCE doesn't know the answers to those questions, then there's absolutely no reason to suppose the answer is to be found in an ancient holy book, or ANY religious text. To believe THAT would be TRUE FUNDAMENTALISM.*"

Another muddying-the-water theist technique is to try to have long, intellectually-formed articles, attempting to describe what an atheist really stands for. "What type of atheist ARE you?" one might say. Materialism, Pantheism, Agnosticism, Negative Theoretic Atheism, Practical Atheism. These are some of the classes of atheism defined. They tell of philosophical differences, and varying levels of commitment towards anti-theism. Suffice-it-to-say that each of these have their basis in history, but you will find that most modern-day atheists are of the 'normal' type, simply enjoying life without the need to believe in an all-knowing super-natural creator, end of story.

A second point to consider regarding accusations of being fundamentalist, are the charges that we are extremists; that we are similar to the people involved in abortion-clinic bombings or the infamous events of Sept. 11th, 2001. These, perhaps, are accusations of the extremely desperate or ill informed, however I feel the need to write on this a bit.

There have been many awful things in our history done in the name of religion, but when have you ever heard of something awful being done in the name of Atheism? It is easy to take out and describe awful things like the extermination of thousands of intellectuals and more by the despotic leader POL POT, for example, and say he did these awful things BECAUSE he was an atheist. In his early beginnings, because of poor grades in school, he was considered to be a prime candidate for inclusion into the anti-intellectual PCF group but that was 20 years before he came to power. I suppose that being an 'anti-intellectual' organization accounts for their targeting of atheists, as a large percentage of true atheists do indeed have (or possess in some way) an intellectual mind-set. POL POT obviously did not. Furthermore, POL POT was into many things, and if you take a reasoned look into his life, he was more about killing people randomly and causing trouble in the name of groups within his country rather than killing people BECAUSE he was an atheist. If he WAS an atheist, he was certainly NOT killing people based on that minor personal belief. He was a nut, pure-and-simple!

The same can be said of STALIN, another person often lumped in with the few despots the world has had to contend with who 'happened to be' atheists (in varying degrees, I might add), but did NOT commit their crimes BECAUSE they were atheists. He was an evil man who had a position of power and was a puppet of LENIN. He was a totalitarian dictator and if he had killed religious people, it would be because they would surely be 'against the state' and thereby against him as well. Further research into Stalin's life reveals that perhaps he was not so anti-theist as people think. In the documentary "Mysteries of the Century: Kremlin Kids" (featuring Stalin's daughter, Svetlana Alliluyeva Stalin) she recalled the following: "*In father's library, between other books, were few tomes of 'Christ.' It was history of Christ written by vox populist Morozov. I said to my father: "But Christ didn't exist!" and he answered, "Oh no, Christ, surely existed.*" She goes on to talk about a few acts that would seem to suggest Stalin was rather soft on dealing with the religious-minded. Under Stalin's insisting. The "*Politburo of the Central Committee has admitted prosecutions of believers "inexpedient". Stalin also "canceled Lenin's instruction from May, 1st, 1919 for N 13666-2 about struggle against priests and religion and gave orders to People's Commissariat of Internal Affairs (NKVD) to release from custody already arrested priests "if activity of these citizens didn't harm the Soviet authority.*"

To all theists who think they will have atheists squirming in their chairs regarding their accusations of past dictators killing religious folk, consider the following. In Stalin's life, before World war two, he killed off most of the Soviet elite. Does that mean he was anti-Soviet? He killed Communists like they were going out of style. Does that mean he was anti-Communist? No, surely not. The actions taken by these despots were horrific, but their attachment to atheism needs to be judged by how they felt about their own personal beliefs, not the coincidental offing of certain groups of people and labeling the killers 'anti-so-and-so'. The logic does not hold true.

The 9/11 tragedy was committed by 19 hijackers who did all "in the name of religion." They "*honestly and sincerely believed they were behaving in a good and righteous fashion*", explains Richard Dawkins. "*They believed they were doing what their god wanted them to do, they believed they were going to a 'martyrs' reward.*" "*There is a logical progression towards extreme religious indoctrination and these types of tragic events. Atheist's beliefs have no such kind of logical, terrible consequences. These Muslim extremist folks have been taught these kinds of things since childhood in their faith schools. If there WERE a school of faith for atheism there most certainly would NOT be any teachings which would demand a violent attack on people. If there WERE such schools they would be taught 'critical-thinking' and how to make up their own minds.*"

Another accusation placed upon atheists (more so on the more vocal ones like the people I refer to in this book) is the way in which they use words to explain their case. Theists will say that they are using the 'language of extremism' in trying to get their facts across. In fact, this so-called 'new atheism' is the current phrase being bandied about on the debate circuit. Some of the more vocal of the atheistic protagonists, Richard Dawkins and

Christopher Hitchens as examples, are accused by various and sundry as being 'militant', 'dogmatic', 'radical', or 'extremist' in their views.

The funny thing about all this (if you can call it 'funny') is the huge gap in the actual extremism practiced, when comparing other social movements like ISLAM, CHRISTIANITY and the BLACK PANTHERS. From http://saintgasoline.com we see that "*What is being branded as 'Extremism,' 'Militance,' and 'Fundamentalism' in the New Atheist movement is hardly analogous to the extremism found in most other social movements. In Islam, for instance, the Extremists talk of destroying infidels and western society, strap bombs to themselves, and fly planes into buildings. In Christianity today, extremists and fundamentalists vilify homosexuals and the reproductive choices of women, often attempting to curtail their rights through legislation. In the civil rights movement, groups like the Black Panthers advocated and even practiced violence. Meanwhile, in the New Atheist movement at worst you might find Hitchens making a smug remark, and that is what constitutes 'atheist fundamentalism' and 'extremism' to so many critics of this movement.*" Passion for the effort and work, plus the energy and enthusiasm observed with these two atheists is often mistaken for an extreme standpoint, but is misguided as you can see.

Another debate topic is the thought, by some theists, that atheists are really agnostics-in-disguise. They go on to accuse atheists of being close-minded in their beliefs and that agnosticism is a more acceptable viewpoint. It is, however, false to accept the view that being agnostic is the middle ground between theism and atheism. Agnostics simply state that they cannot claim to know for sure if any gods exist or not. Atheists simply have an absence of belief in any god. In this way, agnosticism is completely compatible with both theism and atheism. A person can believe in a god (theism) without claiming to know for sure if that god exists; the result is agnostic theism. On the other hand, a person can disbelieve in gods (atheism) without claiming to know for sure that no gods can or do exist; the result is agnostic atheism. The fact is that it is entirely possible for a person to be agnostic AND atheist at the same time. The assertion by theists that atheists are more closed-minded than agnostics hardly is a point in their favor. If atheists are closed-minded for their rejection of gods then, by very definition, so are the theists for their views on the actual existence of gods!

Far be it for atheists to actually be closed-minded to the existence of god though. It is evident that some theists WANT their atheistic opponents to admit that they are agnostic, as they can then accuse them of not being absolutely certain that god exists and of having a faith position and therefore have the upper hand in debates, as that assertion would make the theists feel more comfortable. There are really two definitions of atheism that are considered in this topic. The theist version of an atheist is one who is certain there is no god, whereas the Agnostic is not certain. The atheist version is one who BELIEVES there is no god, whereas an Agnostic simply does not know. I realize the two sound similar, but the reason most atheists say they don't BELIEVE in a god indicates something less than an absolute certainty of a god's nonexistence. In my opinion, any reasonably intelligent atheist would admit that he/she would allow 2 or 3 percentage points in favor of the 'possibility' that there may be a god. It is not a 'sitting-on-the-fence' scenario; rather it is an intelligent, reasoned view based on their understanding of the work science contributes to the world. It is the truth brought about by the 'balance of evidence' (rather than a faith-based position) that motivates atheists. They are aware that some piece of evidence might show itself in the future, and they respect that possibility (again, evidence). At any rate, theists are always trying to find that angle to make the atheistic side more vulnerable, but nothing seems to be doing the trick so far.

One of the main underlying topics of debate surely would have to include the way both science, and religion, view the world. In a religious worldview it's the supernatural concept of existence that is the starting-point for peoples morals and outlook on life, whereas that is not present in a non-religious world-view.

That is the basic premise, however theologians are often too quick to point out, according to www.teachingaboutreligion.org (in the self-interest of their debating position) that "*A world view is acquired on an ongoing basis, and many an individual's worldview framework blends religious notions and practices he or she acquires from a multitude of experiences over time. A person with exposure to several religious traditions is likely to have a life outlook that is "cobbled" from the varied experiences and understandings to which they have been exposed.*"

Although that statement might be true enough, it does not take into account the absolute majority of people who lazily go by the one-and-only religion in which they have been brought up. To suggest that most have such an objective view of their own religion is to suggest that most apply REASON to their religious beliefs and that does not seem to be justifiable. The quote says "a person with exposure to several religious traditions". Where ARE these people? Certainly not in the bible belt of the United States; certainly not in North Korea; freedom of religion does not exist in Saudi Arabia and a lot of other Islamic states. According to www.pewforum.org, referring to the Pentecostal arm of Christianity. "*At least a quarter of the world's 2 billion Christians are thought to be members of these lively, highly personal faiths, which emphasize such spiritually renewing "gifts of the Holy Spirit" as speaking in tongues, divine healing and prophesying. Even more than other Christians, Pentecostals and other Renewalists believe that God, acting through the Holy Spirit, continues to play a direct, active role in everyday life."* I think this quote goes a long way to explaining the real-life view of the believer in our present-day society. Add the fact that (from www.religioustolerance.org) *"Over 33% of the world is Christian, Muslims account for almost 20%, Hindus 13% and 21% of the worlds population practices all the other forms of religion"*, and one gets a pretty clear picture of the sheer numbers. I would LOVE to know what percentage of these people are 'free-thinkers' when it comes to encompassing other peoples 'world-views'?

Some of the debates and discussions are one-sided. These theists are there not to learn anything, but are there to do the preaching they know all too well. Debates are a two-way street and one should always have a little bit of an open mind when entering into such a debate. Preparation should be mandatory, but so should a willingness to learn nuances of the other sides position that, possibly, you were before of unaware.

At a recent debate at a local auditorium, I had the good fortune of being able to pose a question (spoken as a comment because I did not want to come across TOO harsh) to the theists on the stage. I simply asked whether their statements on their actual belief in the existence of god were genuine, or did they simply reflect the fact that they had much to gain from having dedicated a life to religion and religious studies and having written books and profited greatly by their publishing etc. I also stated that would seem a normal and noble thing, to defend oneself against an onslaught of criticism over views tightly held, but that all statements made SHOULD be done with a nod to common-sense and reason, things NOT seemingly high on the agenda of the theistic side. In fact, a reasoned self-look into ones own religious beliefs may trouble many a believer, so naturally we don't expect their arguments to contain much critical-thinking.

I never really did get a satisfactory response to my question that afternoon. Maybe a bit too harsh?

CHAPTER Four

'Thank God' I'm an Atheist

A little history of skepticism (light version)

The title of this chapter was meant to be facetious, as you can guess. "Thank god I'm an atheist" simply refers to the fact that if there were no religion, I would hardly waste my time talking about a subject that would be nonexistent in the first place. One can hardly be non-theistic if there are no religions to be THEISTIC about! Also, It could be said that a book about atheism would have to talk about religion as well. True, and I do bring it up as I see fit. 4,000 years of religion cannot be ignored. It is our history, like it or not. Within my own opinions on atheism versus religion, I will (as I have already done) include it here as I see it pertains to the current area of discussion.

A book about Atheism, the controversies and the theory of evolution, would hardly be considered complete were it not for a chapter that delved into exactly what it is that makes one an ATHEIST. I suppose anyone can guess how difficult it must have been for the first atheist to admit his beliefs to any person. The world in ancient times was just beginning to struggle to understand its place in the universe, and came up with some pretty bizarre concepts (at least by today's standards) to justify those beliefs, and a lot of people relied on those beliefs on the gods to explain what they were seeing and experiencing.

The term ATHEISM (from http://www.wikipedia.org) came from the Greek Atheos meaning 'without gods', which was applied with a negative connotation to those thought to reject the gods worshiped by the larger society." It is, indeed, interesting to see that it was nearly impossible to display one's atheistic beliefs in the relatively primitive world. If you were to travel back in time you would be hard-pressed to find the 'village atheist' anywhere you looked. The simple reason is that, even like now, early societies' religious beliefs were very closely associated with authority and power. You might say that the beliefs of the village elders were the beliefs of everyone else too. As societies became more complex and organized, the concept of patriotism would also influence many of the community's members towards the popular existing beliefs of the time.

An intelligent observation, this time from LUCIOS ANNAEUS SENECA the younger (4-65 CE) is as follows, and sums up nicely the way religion has been, in my opinion, ever since the start:

"Religion is regarded by the common people as true, by the wise as false, and by the rulers as useful." And THAT was from 2,000 years ago. Amazing.

In ancient Greece, one would hardly want to venture out into the town square and denounce all gods. The routine, religiously speaking, *"was to believe in the gods (Apollo, Ares, Artemis, Athena, Demeter, Dionysus, Hades, Hephaestus, Hera, Hermes, Hestia, Poseidon, and the one-and-only Zeus) and perform the proper sacrifices and rituals,"* thereby avoiding any problems both from gods and fellow human beings and encourage gifts from the gods. The Greeks also believed in the afterlife. Ancient China had the same kind of worship rituals, and the inhabitants worshipped many different gods. There are currently about 154 Chinese deities on record (some had multiple names) spanning many centuries. Australia had around 78, Africa reached almost 195 and famous Egypt laid claim to about 173 deities.

It was around the time we now know as ancient Greece that the idea of somehow challenging the notion of the existence of gods came into being. It was taken for granted that everyone believed in the gods of the day, however it was probably a bit easier to HAVE atheistic thoughts then (if one could call them that) as there was no church in pagan antiquity, and therefore no-one to really feel threatened by someone claiming non-belief in the gods. So there was no punishment or rebuke towards those early atheists.

These early philosophers ranged in their belief-systems. Xenophanes "*chastised the human vices*" of the gods, whereas Aristotle thought there was a 'prime-mover' which had "*set creation going, but was not connected or interested in the universe.*" A well-known (and my personal favorite), famous argument against the existence of god or gods was the RIDDLE OF EPICURUS. Epicurus was another of the ancient Greek philosophers and wrote: "*God either wants to eliminate bad things and cannot, or can but does not want to, or neither wishes to nor can, or both wants to and can. If he wants to and cannot, then he is weak - and this does not apply to god. If he can but does not want to, then he is spiteful - which is equally foreign to god's nature. If he neither wants to nor can, he is both weak and spiteful, and so not a god. If he wants to and can, which is the only thing fitting for a god, where then do bad things come from? Or why does he not eliminate them?*" Variants of this line of thought continue up to this day.

Around 500 A.D. you start to see the overwhelming influence of the Catholic faith, which was, by now, the dominant religion of the Roman Empire. As the older Greek schools of philosophy were closed down by the Roman-Catholic faith, they effectively eliminated the threat of a rational, materialist view of the universe that some of the Greeks put forward. What is notable here is that, for centuries after, you had a huge mass of ordinary people that could not read nor write (with the exception of the nobility, the church and the people that 'ran' things) and so it is virtually impossible to find any record of what the 'everyday man' would have been thinking with regards to the existence of god, and religion. The masses only had the word of the priests of the day and an enormous array of sacred imagery to learn from, many of them depicting the various stories from the bible, and often found adorning places of worship as frescoes. If these pictures were one of the few sources of religious knowledge for the majority of the inhabitants of Medieval Europe, plus the fact that science was in its infancy, no wonder hardly any real anti-theist opinions flourished. This period of our history (roughly AD 480-1,000) has been labeled the 'DARK AGES'. Many definitions have been given for this title, but the usual one refers to *"the intellectual darkness of the times where there was a scarcity of sound literature and cultural achievements."*

Things started to change around the 15th century, as more and more people realized that, among other things, they had the ability to travel worldwide, and that there were OTHER society's that did not have the same belief systems. Some countries didn't even have Christianity as their faith!!! As noted, the Christian Roman empire was successful in closing down the old schools of philosophy (under the orders of the Emperor Justinian) and, after doing so, simply discarded those works of Aristotle (and others) that showed an allegiance to anything other than pure religious faith and a belief in a god. If this was where it stopped, then it is anyone's guess how much MORE religious we all would have become, were it not for the Arabic scholars (in the Middle east, then later, Spain) who revived that materialistic view of the universe. They had preserved the complete works of Aristotle. The important idea here is that these scholars translated these works into Latin and were spread throughout Christian Europe, where the first real atheists created some of the arguments we know today.

As we are climbing up the historical tree of atheism and religion, we find ourselves now at the end of the so-called 'Dark ages' and at the period from about 1,000-1,600 A.D. I don't want to drag this out but it IS an interesting time in the development of atheistic thought. It was at this time that the CRUSADES, or "*series of religiously-sanctioned military campaigns waged by much of Latin Christian Europe were let loose in an attempt to restore Christian control to the holy land.*" Ultimately, there were other later crusades that did NOT have the sanction of the pope, and they were due to internal fighting amongst the political and Christian powers of the day.

As stated before, to be a non-theist back then was surely a death-sentence, and even the famous scientist Galileo (imprisoned for the rest of his life for daring to postulate that perhaps our little planet was NOT the center of the universe) and one of his biggest followers, Giordano Bruno (tortured for 8 years then burned alive in a Roman flower market in 1,600) did not escape religious persecution.. There were several different 'sects' of Christianity, fairly considered to be atheistic in thought that were borne out of this period in history. The biggest one were the UNITARIANS who, even today, state that "*We welcome people who identify with and draw inspiration from Atheism and Agnosticism, Buddhism, Christianity, Humanism, Judaism, Paganism, and other religious or philosophical traditions.*" Critical thinking, indeed! However, burnings-at-the-stake were still quite common, so it would be very difficult to find anyone openly opposing theism or calling themselves an atheist for the obvious consequences. Many people ended up simply denying accusations. Some were successful. Others were not.

This was an unusual period of accusations and denials and it is worth noting that during this time it was the practice of the church to DENY the existence of atheism. Strange, then, that the very people who are denying atheism were the same folks who were torturing people they believed to BE atheists! This went on for nearly 200 years! Simon Schaffer, professor of the history and philosophy of science at Cambridge University, sums it up nicely: "*There is this extraordinarily interesting ambiguity in which some of the most ferocious 'atheism hunters' of the 16th, 17th, and 18th centuries can simultaneously be found saying that there's no such thing as atheists, because one of the best arguments that the enemies of any denial of gods existence have going for them is that it is impossible so to do, and therefore a very good argument AGAINST atheists is that there aren't any.*" He goes on to say "*So the high stakes for which the game is played, lead to this absolutely fascinating logical problem, that one is denying the existence of the position against which one is arguing*"....... Priceless.

One example of just how strange this time was in studying the history of religious attitudes and atheism is a quote from a very popular French Catholic theologian, a priest, by the name of Pierre Charron (1541-1603). This is a statement from his book on wisdom. "*All religions have this in common, that they are an outrage in common-sense, for they are pieced together out of a variety of evidence, some of which seems so unworthy, sordid, and at odds with man's reason, that any strong and vigorous intelligence laughs at them."*

By the end of the 18th century, deism (the belief in gods) in England was lessening slightly, however the French philosopher VOLTAIRE was the one mainly responsible for conveying deist ideas throughout Europe. The relationship between atheism and theism in France at that time was 'heating up', so-to-speak, as 7 major books about non-theistic thought were burned publicly on August 18th, 1770 by the 'official executioner'. 3 of those books were written under a pseudonym, and we now know the authors name. He was the Baron Pierre Henri D. Holbach (1723-1789), and is reasonably credited with writing the first, true all-atheist book. He did not accept the fact that there was a 'first-cause' to the universe, nor did he ascribe to the beliefs that the soul was 'immortal'. This set him apart from most other writers of his day as they would sometimes adopt a 'sitting-on-the-fence' approach to these issues. His book (now called the 'atheist bible') contains an amazing quote from this person.. Another one of my favorites, and here it is:

"If we go back to the beginning we shall find that ignorance and fear created the gods; that fancy, enthusiasm or deceit, adorned them: that weakness worshiped them; that credulity preserves them, and that custom, respect and tyranny support them, in order to make the blindness of men serve their own interests. If the ignorance of nature gave BIRTH to gods, the KNOWLEDGE of nature is calculated to destroy them."

One little-known example of how a modern-age leader's views towards atheists highlights the potential struggle we have before us, and one that exemplifies the difficulties that a primitive non-believer must have had way back when, is from an exchange between the former senior President

George Bush and an accredited reporter and member of the press corps Robert L Sherman. From http://www.e-thepeople.org we get the transcript:

Sherman: "*What will you do to win the votes of the Americans who are Atheists?*"

Bush: "*I guess I'm pretty weak in the Atheist community. Faith in god is important to me.*"

Sherman: "*Surely you recognize the equal citizenship and patriotism of Americans who are Atheists?*"

Bush: "*No, I don't know that Atheists should be considered as citizens, nor should they be considered patriots. This is one nation under God.*"

Sherman (somewhat taken aback): "*Do you support as a sound constitutional principle the separation of state and church?*"

Bush: "*Yes, I support the separation of church and state. I'm just not very high on Atheists.*"

The leader of the free world, ladies and gentlemen.

These statements by the former President might appear out-of-place for yet ANOTHER reason and one in which I have touched on already, namely that when America declared its independence in 1776 it was stated that there would be absolute separation of church and state. It is therefore hard to believe why religion today has (or seems to have) a majority stake in our Congress, 100%!! That's right, not one non-believer among 'em! To be fair, there are religious denominations that are both under and over-represented in Congress, so in a way I guess it all balances itself out? NO. The fact that the U.S. Congress is not representative of the American public-at-large in this way is troubling. However, 44 percent of the House and

Senate are millionaires whereas only one percent of Americans are, so.

At any rate, it might be worth pointing out, however, that our first president, George Washington, never really like going to church and often left before the sacrament was given. When chastised for this by the local priest, he agreed that these frequent, early departures would most likely set a bad example to the rest of the parishioners, so he never went to church again! Quite a number of succeeding presidents were, on record, also considerably less than 'devout' Christians.

Here are some quotes from some of those early Presidents and founding fathers. The first is one from John Adams, the second President of the United States. "*God is an essence we know nothing of. Until this awful blasphemy's got rid of, there will never be any liberal science in the world.*" This one is from Thomas Jefferson, the third President. "*The clergy believe that any power confided in me, would be exerted in opposition to their schemes. And they believe rightly.*" "*I have seldom met an intelligent person whose views were not narrowed and distorted by religion.*" This last one was by the 15th President of the United States, James Buchanan. I cite these examples simply to show that at least SOME of our illustrious leaders were on the right track.

Oh, okay, here is another one for you, just in case you were 'chomping-at-the-bit'. Abraham Lincoln stated, "*My earlier views on the unsoundness of the Christian scheme of salvation have become clearer, and stronger, with advancing years.*"

Having an openly non-theist position today is relatively easy. We have far freer societies and laws that try to protect the rights of groups and individuals. Our right to practice religion (or to have non at all) is there for all to enjoy. It could be stated as well that the increase in the percentage of non-believers could be attributed to the technologically advanced world in which we live. We are surrounded by all the comforts one could imagine. Dinners that can be made in two minutes; communication devices that allow instant contact between friends and family; traveling around the world in less time that it probably took a horse and cart to go to market in times past. All these things could be seen to take the place of the consolation and comfort one could possibly get from religion in an ancient society. Today there just doesn't seem much real use for it. The people who need our world's religions to continue today are the folks who make lots of money off it. The power-elite and the politically-connected all claim to have some connection to the 'almighty', even if it is just 'politically-correct to say so. I am sure that (in a thousand years, lol , when we are all atheists), one would not expect a presidential candidate to get on stage extolling the virtues of the resurrection and the second coming! That would be political suicide.

Of course there are people that feel genuinely stuck to the religious 'round-about' and don't even consider getting off. All the more power to them. It is not possible to ignore the entrenchment of religion over the past 4,000 years across the globe, but it is also easy to see, even in the brief glimpse of the history of atheism seen above, that the general primitive ignorance and powerlessness of our descendants made them ripe for indoctrination into such a religious belief system. It also shows that where there used to be power and money (and where religion called all the shots) it was a way of life for people for many centuries. It was only after more people started getting educated, started traveling further afield and began witnessing differing points of view on life, that they could finally start (very carefully) to think critically for themselves. "*We have the ancient Greek philosophers to thank for that. We have the free thinkers of the Renaissance period to thank for that. We have the 'age of enlightenment' to thank for that.*" We also have Charles Darwin and his followers to thank for that. In the present day we have a whole lot of intellectual and scientific folks armed with reason and hopefully one day, more people will actually, and simply, 'GET IT'.

Chapter Five

Logic only a Theist could conjure

Here is the first of three chapters spread throughout this book dedicated solely to the up-and-coming debater who might like to see some of the most popular arguments for the existence of god, and my refutations of them. I, personally, find it hard to comment on most of the ones in THIS chapter as they all seem to have a common thread (the assumption that there is a GOD (the Judeo-Christian one, of course) and that he/she/it is the 'prime mover' of the universe. That conclusion is reached even before the 'proofs' are on the table! More arguments later and a chapter on 'questions for atheists' I personally find more entertaining, but these here need to be mentioned, as theists eventually bring them up.

"*The arguments below are not meant to demonstrate gods existence conclusively, nor are they equal in their strengths,*" according to the author. All rely on psychology and some on cosmology. Some are quite popular and have similar basis in theme and in logic, but I will paraphrase to make them digestible for all. I will be using the website http://www.peterkreeft.com for the source listing of these arguments. Peter Kreeft is a professor of philosophy at Boston College and at the King's College (Empire State Building), in New York City. He is an author, in-demand speaker and Christian apologist.

Let me digress and again mention why I would even want to debate a theist in the first place. I really do not have any negativity to lay on the unwitting theist. I also have no intentions of converting them to my simple 'God-less' belief. No, the only real reason I have to debate theists is to try to get them along the critical-thinking path. If I can get them to use one ounce of reason and apply that to some of their beliefs, I would be one happy camper. To be real, most atheists would rather simply talk among themselves rather than go head-to-head with a theist. We all know pretty well that their side will have nothing more than statements of philosophy and meta-physics than anything tangible. Even among those highly intellectual religious debaters one only gets slightly more well-packaged forms of the same old things. You have read in this book that some people think atheism is a religion or a radically different philosophy of thought. This is yet another reason why atheists like to debate theists, to dispel any misconceptions about this. Let's move on.

One telling trait of Mr. Kreeft's opening introduction before he discusses his pro-god arguments is the fact that he all but admits proving god's existence is most improbable, or at the very least, unlikely. "*We realize that many people, both believers and nonbelievers, doubt that God's existence can be demonstrated or even argued about.*" Well, I would say that non-believers would tend to agree with that, don't you? He goes on to intimate that these arguments (about god's existence) are only a passing thought and that at least "*attention to these arguments has its place in any book on apologetics.*" He goes on to intimate that these arguments are really only for those of 'us' that are "*looking for some reason, beyond the assurances of Scripture, to believe that there is more.*

Well, the 'more', surely, to which he is referring, is the very simple proof and evidence that we are all after! I hope he does not expect the intellect of our world's inhabitants to go south and blindly accept these primitive teachings without questioning the content? When was all this stuff written and by whom? There are many questions you should be asking. Again, he does not seem to place too much importance in these arguments, as though they are simply after-thoughts to the whole 'god-belief' debate. The last paragraph before his arguments states that it is the combination of all 20 arguments, in part of a cumulative case that is most effective, and that each one contributes differently to the story. Most seem to be simply variations on a theme to me. But I'll let you be the judge.

With that in mind, here are some of the 20 arguments as presented by Peter Kreeft (paraphrasing here and there for expediency) and my arguments against them.

One) THE ARGUMENT FROM CHANGE

This one is definitely from the psychological camp. The gist of the argument is that one cannot have change (say in the growth of a tree or a human) without external help. Some other 'moving' source has to act on it (in the case of a tree- sunlight, water, etc.) in order for an acorn to get to a full-sized oak tree, for example. In discussing the universe in this context he sums up "*The universe is the sum total of all these moving things, however many there are. The whole universe is in the process of change. But we have already seen that change in any being requires an outside force to actualize*

48

it. Therefore, there is some force outside (in addition to) the universe, some real being transcendent to the universe. This is one of the things meant by 'God.'"

My two cents

Again this argument may have a legitimate grounding in logic, however there are assumptions made that need to be addressed. The most blatant assumption is that one needs to define a singular transcendent entity as being responsible for creating the universe. Maybe there was a team of 'transcendents' to do all that work. To compare the sun and rain, two natural ingredients the earth naturally possesses, with a divine creator is a leap indeed. The rain forms and the sun is ever-present and brings life to our planet. Without these 2 things at least, and more, we would not be here. Who is to say the universe has not always existed? Even if it has not the leap that because he says everything needs an outside causation does nothing to bolster the theist side to suggest a supreme being had anything to do with the creation of it. Since our minds cannot comprehend a never-ending, always-here universe, we better just put this argument to rest. You will see a similar theme in the next few arguments.

TWO) THE ARGUMENT FROM EFFICIENT CAUSALITY

My brain imploded on this one, but I will try to paraphrase so even I can get more of a handle on what the author is trying to get at. Similar to the first argument this one is trying to state that everything that exists needs something around it to support it, to make it exist. We are all already here, so we do have a network of things in place to keep, intact, our existence. I'll use his direct quote from one of his paragraphs, as perhaps it explains things better than I could. His example begins with: "*Suppose we needed 7 things to keep us in existence. Then suppose those 7 things needed still MORE things to keep THEM in existence, for without those, we would not exist. If there is nothing besides that universe of changing, dependent things, then the Universe, and you as part of it could not be. For everything that is would right now need to be given being but there would be nothing capable of giving it. And yet you are and it is. So there must in that case exist something besides the universe of dependent things, something not dependent as they are."*

Again, this argument seems to assume an awful lot. It is quite easy to see how our lives and everything on our planet needs external forces to keep us in existence. We need the sun, water, food, the support of other people, money, and the list goes on. The argument bases it's hopes on the fact that it is intended to show that the only way for anything to have come into existence in the first place, is to have an 'uncaused cause.' That would be the one explanation of how this universe got started, and would thus continue to explain how we needed to initially have directed causation otherwise we would all not be here. Again, assumptions of the universe springing into existence and of GOD being that external being that is independent of our universe are still here, and these assumptions usually tend to make these arguments weak. There is also the discussion of 'infinite causal regression'. I bring this to the table only to state that if there were an infinite regress of causes to our existence then the scientific community could not ever hope to come up with anything solid about the supposed 'beginnings' of our universe because, if this were true, there would be no beginning! The corollary to that, of course, would be an uplifting HURRAH!! from the atheist camp as that would put to bed any idea of an 'uncaused cause' creating the first speck in the heavens, and that we have always been here, ad infinitum. Again, more metaphysics from the theist side; always moving away from empirical, quantifiable facts and evidence.

THREE) THE ARGUMENT FROM TIME AND CONTINGENCY

This is one of the more famous arguments, and AGAIN assumes that once-upon-a-time there was nothing in existence. In fact, the only chance this argument has of surviving is if we all agree that there really was nothing before the universe began. I just had a thought wash over me that we will never arrive at a conclusion regarding the origins of our universe. My feeling is that the discussion of it will simply be the fodder of intellectual think tanks and fireside debates forever. I, personally, can only stick to my guns and state that the invention of a god for the beginnings of our universe is just as silly an idea as can be thought up by us here on earth, as anything else. I'll always be on the side of the theoretical physicists and others that attempt to explain curved space and black holes with event horizons. I digress again. Back to contingency we go.

Typically, this argument also bases it's conclusions on assumptions that there needs to be a non-contingent being to start what we all see, hear, and feel. The basic argument offers that it is a real possibility that nothing COULD have existed. It is one of those possibilities that, If we were to go back in time 909 billion years and it was assumed that nothing existed, then that state could continue forever, with nothing ever existing (of course there would be no-one around to confirm that). It continues to argue that since that possibility did not happen (that the universe DID begin), and that it is impossible to get something from nothing, then there has to be something ultimately that does not need anything to justify it's existence; a 'necessary' being to put things in motion; something that cannot NOT exist. This thing, therefore, is God. I would like to include a segment of Mr. Kreef's final paragraph here, seemingly taking things a bit further.

"But if non-being is a real possibility for you, then you are the kind of being that cannot last forever. In other words, the possibility of non-being must be built-in, "programmed," part of your very constitution, a necessary property. And if all being is like that, then how could anything still exist after the passage of an infinite time? For an infinite time is every bit as long as forever. So being must have what it takes to last forever, that is, to stay in existence for an infinite time. Therefore there must exist within the realm of being something that does not tend to go out of existence. And this sort of being, as Thomas Aquinas says, is called "necessary."

Unfortunately, Mr. Kreeft seems to be taking this argument too far, and extending it past where we, and our surroundings, no longer exist. If we no longer exist, I would think it academic that there exist a divine, Supreme Being at all. He certainly would have no subjects on whom to claim dominion. I do understand his assertion that we are finite beings and that we do need outside elements in which to exist, however the great leap STILL, in this argument and with the ones listed so far, is the notion that the universe had a beginning and therefore, a creator. This has never been proved. Also, there is a large body of theories and evidence to support the idea of a naturally occurring universe, even though we do not know for sure how it all began (if it ever did). Let's face it, ANYONE with a fertile imagination can come up with a mystical 'being' that magically created and controls our universe. This lame argument STILL presupposes that a God is a necessary, perpetual being, and that without 'him' we would not exist. Still waiting for the proof folks.

This might have held up hundreds of years ago when the possibility of an infinite universe was not even considered, however with today's advancements in science these old arguments will have to be tweaked a bit if they expect to convince anyone, especially a non-believer.

FOUR) THE ARGUMENT FROM DEGREES OF PERFECTION

This one is hardly worth the ink this sentence will hopefully be made of when published. The whole argument suggests that in life there are more perfect beings than others (ones who can give and receive love are better than ones who cannot) and that in this scale of 'perfectness' it would follow that a 'best' would exist somewhere who would be "*a source and real standard of all the perfections that we recognize belong to us as beings.*" The writer confidently continues that "*this absolutely perfect being, the "Being of all beings," "the Perfection of all perfections, is God.*" He goes on to state "*the argument assumes a real "better." But aren't all our judgments of comparative value merely subjective?*"

Here is the way I would end the discussion of the above argument. Why stop at 'perfectness' as being the barometer by which we all are compared? Why not use various levels of 'stupidity' as our guide? In this hypothetical 'scale of stupidity' it would also then follow that a 'best' would exist somewhere who would be " a source and real standard of all the 'stupidness' that we recognize belong to us as beings." To conclude in his logical progression we might have, "This absolutely stupid being", the "being of all beings", "the stupidest of all the stupids", is God. No proof........ again.

Ahh yes. Subjectivity; the bane of the theist's existence. Of course all of history and the peoples within our planet can confirm the OBJECTIVITY of God's existence. We have had many hundreds, even thousands of gods from which to choose. Why NOT believe in the Judeo-Christian one? Only kidding. Again, folks, this is way too much of a stretch and can be discarded immediately.

FIVE) THE DESIGN ARGUMENT

I won't go over this one yet. We will have a bit of fun with it later. And the theists are so SERIOUS when they offer it to us. Really amusing.

SIX) THE KALAM ARGUMENT

Evidently, the Kalam argument is one that has been studied and still contributes to the Christian way of belief in god. It's kind of long-winded, but here is the upshot. It does seem similar to the above, but here it is anyway. First, it gives us three axioms. These are:

1) *Whatever begins to exist has a cause for its coming into being.*

2) *The universe began to exist.*

3) *Therefore, the universe has a cause for its coming into being.*

Let's deal with this first, and then try to take apart the more detailed statements this argument has. Number one I would have to agree with. I can't think of anything that spontaneously comes into existence without some external force acting upon it in some fashion. Here again we have the old assumption in number two that the universe had a beginning. The writer tries to prove it later on.... hold on; we're getting there. Number three obviously assumes that number two is correct then portends to make a conclusion based on that assumption. Naughty-naughty.

Here is the author, as he continues to try to explain how an infinite universe cannot be.

"Is the second premise true? Did the universe, the collection of all things bounded by space and time, begin to exist? This premise has recently received powerful support from natural science, from so-called Big Bang Cosmology. But there are philosophical arguments in its favor as well. Can an infinite task ever be done or completed? If, in order to reach a certain end, infinitely many steps had to precede it, could the end ever be reached? Of course not. Not even in an infinite time. For an infinite time would be unending, just as the steps would be. In other words, no end would ever be reached. The task would, could never be completed."

He seems to revel in the fact that he can talk his way through the concept of infinite time and prove to us that the universe MUST have had a beginning. ALL theists need this to be true otherwise their 'creation' theory falls apart in spades. The man continues:

"Now if the universe never began, then it always was. If it always was, then it is infinitely old. If it were infinitely old, then an infinite amount of time would have to have elapsed before (say) today. And so an infinite number of days must have been completed, one day succeeding another, one bit of time being added to what went before, in order for the present day to arrive. But this exactly parallels the problem of an infinite task. If the present day has been reached, then the actually infinite sequence of history has

reached this present point: in fact, has been completed up to this point for at any present point the whole past must already have happened. But an infinite sequence of steps could never have reached this present point, or any point before it." And some more:

"*So, either the present day has not been reached, or the process of reaching it was not infinite. But obviously the present day has been reached. So the process of reaching it was not infinite. In other words, the universe began to exist. Therefore, the universe has a cause for its coming into being, a Creator.*"

So what we simply have here are two major assumptions, with not one shred of evidence or proof. The first assumption is that (through an elegant, well-thought-out argument of how infinity cannot exist) the Universe is finite. The second is that, since it is finite, there must be a creator and that creator must be god. I find it amusing that I always seem to be back at square one after hearing all these religious 'proofs'.

Time is very difficult to define. Some scientists would say it is the observed process of changing things. Others have shown that a clock would behave differently on other planets and within other galaxies. From where, then, do we get our concept of time? We are lucky that the earth rotates as it does, for it allows us to get a decent sleep at night and a decent day in which to work, play, etc. If one is going to create an argument using time and space, one had better do the research before postulating an argument. In this case, it is better that the non-believer does his/her homework so a clear rebuttal can be executed.

In actual fact, the author's concept of time is a major flaw with his thesis. This last part of his argument seems to hinge on his concept of time as being linear in form. Even though there are many scientists and mathematicians working on this subject, as an interesting topic of discussion I submit that time is only linear to us, as we observe it from a fixed point on our planet. Some say, I believe correctly, that time does not exist. Things only exist and change in space, not time. We call a day a day, but in reality all that has happened is yet another rotation of our earth around its own axis. 'Movement in space'. Some people would say, "*well, yes, the earth took 24 hours to rotate*", however that is still only an objective viewpoint, relative to how we live here on earth. If we were to go to another solar system and the clocks were to go half as fast due to the atmosphere, etc. how do you suppose would we deal with that? No doubt we would invent a way in which we could sleep, eat and work in the fashion we are used to, and come up with a new 'time' that suited us.

Ever think that: "*how on earth can it be Monday in Australia but Sunday in Miami*? That's one earthly example of what I am talking about. Humans created time to fit our society's needs. I say it is the same 'time' in both cities (by that I mean the same instance in 'space'). Because it is darker over in Australia during a part of the earth's rotation should not alter the fact that it is the same 'time' for both places. We have watches and clocks that tick away the hours and minutes and we perceive time in a linear fashion. We cannot go back or forward in time because there is no time to go back into. Things change, that's all. We observe time as a relative function of things changing. We inhabit the planet through many rotations of our earth and we get older. Monday and Tuesday. Different days?? Well, for our functioning society they HAVE to be. In reality, if you were looking at our solar system from one million miles away what would you see? You would see the sun shining continuously (unless your view happened to be blocked) and you would see all these little planets rotating around and around. We, as humans, need to have things compartmentalized and ordered otherwise we could not function. I know it's hard to get your head around that concept because we use TIME so much and we live by it. Existence is real; time is simply perceived. It, on it's own, does not exist, or so I believe, and would thus render the above argument useless because of the very possibility that the universe has existed forever. We simply occupy a little space within it. His statement, then, regarding not being able to 'get' to our present day (in an infinitely progressing universe) would be invalid in this case. We have not 'travelled' to this place in time. We simply occupy this place in space.

Another thought is the way that if one were able to go faster than the speed of light, then one could conceivably go back in time. If you think about it (and I know I am side-slipping, but it is an interesting topic anyway) just because you are going faster than the speed of light only means that what you are perceiving is different. Light does not affect 'time', as I suggest that there is just space, and one just moves about 'within' it. Moving faster than the speed of light would, I assume, allow us to see absolutely nothing, as the light that reflects off objects, and allows us to see, would be ever in our tail-pipe dust.

Going back in time has it's own set of problems and I am sure most of you are aware of at least some of them; the paradox of going back in time to kill your Great grandfather so that you would not exist in the first place, for example. I am sure you know that one. There are theories that if you COULD go back in time you would simply be in a parallel universe and changing that situation in that alternate universe, therefore sparing your own existence. I only include these paragraphs for interest, and to show that Mr. Kreef's concept of space and time vis-a-vis his 'existence of God' argument needs to be updated to fit present-day (or should I say 'present-space') knowledge. From now on, in the writing of this book, I reserve the right to use 'time' as we all understand it, OK?

SEVEN) THE ARGUMENT FROM CONTINGENCY

We have been-there-and-done-that, so we will leave well enough alone.

EIGHT) THE ARGUMENT FROM THE WORLD AS AN INTERACTING WHOLE

Some thought had to be done in creating this version of the design argument, I must admit. This version is by Norris Clarke, a teacher of metaphysics and philosophy of religion at Fordham. A lot of paraphrasing is called for here, as I don't want to take up TOO much space here, but I DO want to give it a chance.

Starting point: Our world is a very ordered one and responds to the Laws of Nature, as we know them. Oxygen and hydrogen are always in the same proportions, and all other elements are "*ordered to move toward every other according to the fixed proportions of the law of gravity.*" No one component part of our world can operate independently from one another. Our world is a "*tightly interlocking whole, where relationship to the whole structures and determines the parts. The parts can no longer be understood apart from the whole; its influence permeates them all.*"

"*Any one part could be self-sufficient only if it were the cause of the whole rest of the system, which is impossible, since no part can act except in collaboration with the others.*" And this is where the argument dissolves. IT STILL ASSUMES THERE IS A 'CONTINGENT' BEING RESPONSIBLE FOR OUR UNIVERSE! We continue with his conclusions.

1) "*Since the parts make sense only within the whole, and neither the whole nor the parts can explain their own existence, then such a system as our world requires a unifying efficient cause to posit it in existence as a unified whole.*" That was a direct quote. Notice this writers need for that 'uncaused' cause again?

2) "*This 'unifying element' must be an intelligent one, as it combines the physical laws and all their 'underlying elements'. "To be actually present all at once as a whole this unity can only be the unity of an organizing unifying idea. For only an idea can hold together many different elements at once without destroying or fusing their distinctness.*"

"*Now a real idea cannot actually exist and be effectively operative save in a real mind, which has the creative power to bring such a system into real existence. Hence the sufficient reason for our ordered world-system must ultimately be a creative ordering Mind.*"

3) "*Such an ordering Mind must be independent of the system itself, that is, transcendent; not dependent on the system for its own existence and operation.*"

"*Thus our material universe necessarily requires, as the sufficient reason for its actual existence as an operating whole, a Transcendent Creative Mind.*" WHEW! Glad we all got through that one! Obviously the writer contends that this idea-thinker and doer is the one-and-only GOD.

Again, the main thesis for this argument assumes that there is a creator that does not need a reason for it's being. It is suggesting that we are all part of a grand scheme with all sorts of things acting on and around us to allow us to exist. No argument there, but to not avail oneself of modern-day evidence and theories to explain our natural world is to be closed-minded.

I don't think I need to write a rebuttal here. I call this type of argument 'creeping logic', in that it hopes to convince you of a little bit at a time and then move on to the next leap. As you can see, it appears that most of the arguments so far have assumed that the universe had to have a start. Still not proven one way or the other. The next assumption is that there had to be a divine, transcendent being to do all the work. You KNOW how I feel about that. In case you are thinking that I NEED the universe to always have existed in order to make my position true, you would be mistaken. Whether the universe was made by a 'big-bang' or it has always existed, I can live with both. There is no need to assume external causation of a universe that could be X trillions of years old, or just 15 billion years.

9) THE ARGUMENT FROM MIRACLES (this should be good)

The argument starts this way:

1. *A miracle is an event whose only adequate explanation is the extraordinary and direct intervention of God.* (If you say so)

2. *There are numerous well-attested miracles.* (I would like to see or hear about one that we all conclude is a miracle)

3. *Therefore, there are numerous events whose only adequate explanation is the extraordinary and direct intervention of God.* (Leap of logic, assumes proofs not in evidence).

4. *Therefore God exists.* (Conclusion based on non-proofs and assumptions made on the intervention of the very thing we are trying to determine, namely God's existence. How can you use God in a proof when it is he/she/it that you are trying to prove exists in the first place?)

Well, here are two direct quotes from this argument: "*So there is not really a proof from miracles*". And "*The argument is not a proof, but a very powerful clue or sign.*" To be fair, he states that miracles have to be religious in nature and have to be attributed to some religious authority, but it is usually the religious folks who judge and determine whether a miracle is true or not. Almost like asking the fox to guard the hen house.

Synchronicity, the concept of two or more things happening at the same time with each event having a different 'causation', is a field well studied and suggests that coincidences can happen, and do quite often. Most often the religiously motivated individual will give these events mystifying characteristics and will certainly attribute these happenings as being the work of whatever deity the person worships.

I don't really think I will continue with this one. Isn't there ANY decent argument you people have for god's existence? 100's of millions of people believe in the concept. SO WHERE IS THE PROOF?

Unfortunately, I have to stop here as I read through the remaining 11 arguments and, true-to-form, all I saw was more psychological babble and re-hashing of old arguments that are not worth the effort in which to respond. At least I gave you an idea of the kinds of 'technical' (illogical) arguments their side is putting out. I must also apologize as I was hoping to get far more out of these arguments than I did. I did a fair amount of research into this book, and I honestly did not find ANY one argument for the existence of god where I had to stop and re-read the argument because I thought there was something there to be considered.

All I ask for is one puny bit of evidence.

Chapter Six

Wendy Wright and the Concerned Women of America

(And some scientists that do not believe in evolution either!)

As stated earlier in this book, nothing gives me pleasure in putting someone in a relative 'negative light' as we all have our own opinions and perspectives, and we should all respect each other's viewpoints. However, as Ms. Wendy Wright (President of the Concerned Women of America) engaged Professor Richard Dawkins in a lengthy discussion in 2008 (regarding evolution) and showed her obvious intolerance of the simplest concepts Dawkins had to offer, I felt the need to include her efforts in this book, as her relatively close-minded opinions on evolution mirrors many others. The second point on this is that she represents over 500,000 women in her organization alone; I assume mainly all with a common viewpoint. I suggest that all of you go to YouTube and type in something like *"Richard Dawkins Wendy Wright interview,"* and (if you can get through all 7 of the 10 minute video segments without throwing something at your computer monitor) you win a lollipop! I mean no offense by this short chapter on Ms. Wright, just giving my honest observations from my viewpoint. I realize it is easier to criticize AFTER the fact, and a lot harder to actually DO the interview, but I think a comment on it fits into this discussion quite well.

It may be worth noting here that I have educated myself watching many of Ms. Wright's interviews by way of videos online and on television, and I have found one common thread amongst most. Her lack of knowledge of (or perhaps pure indifference to) the science base on the topic of discussion is incredible. Whether it is a show about stem-cell research or the 'morning-after pill', she uses misstatements about the science to attempt to bolster her position. I truly believe she is doing a disservice to all of her followers and they should get someone more scientifically experienced to appear on these nationally televised shows where science plays an important part.

The first obvious blunder by Ms. Wright is her inability to accept the evidence, as offered by Professor Dawkins. Numerous times Dawkins stated that she only needed to visit one of the major museums in this country to observe the public fossil record to see some very elegant species' progressions. She would always state, "*Show me the fossil evidence.*" The publicly available fossil record for all to see in our museums only represents a minute fraction of the fossil record. Indeed, there are mountains of fossils that may not appear to be attractive enough to be of interest to the general public, but that constitute the bulk of fossils the scientists study. Obviously we can't simply dump auditorium-loads of fossils into museums where only fragments of this and pieces of that will be seen. Scientists know what they are looking at, but the public would be easily bored. Seeing a complete fossil of a dinosaur or an ancient human, now THAT'S fun to see. The museums are not here to bore us. They are here to give us grounding in science and an understanding of what's going on. We'll let the scientists sift through the boring stuff. We want to see the T-REX! I only wished that Professor Dawkins had offered to accompany her to a museum and to explain to her what they would be looking at. Maybe that little bit of an education might allow her to step back and re-asses her position slightly. Otherwise, she seems to be just coming off as another fundamentalist, strictly ignoring the opposing, reasoned-based viewpoint, and blundering through in an awkward manner.

Representing such a large group of women can't be any easy task, but I wonder how much of Ms. Wright's opinions are simply an attempt to 'tow the party line' and throw reason to the wind? Also, It was frustrating to hear her relegating Professor Dawkins to the level of a schoolboy in her classroom, chastising him (or people that believe like him) for having little respect for other people. I mean, does she honestly think that her believing in a 'loving creator' (cut-away to her 'holier-than-thou smirk') gives her a leg-up on respecting other people? She STARTED the 'no respect' conversation! The fact that she had an agenda was obvious to anyone that breathes, yet, upon Dawkin's attempt at nudging that information from her, she quickly snapped that he "*was using ad-hominem*" attacks against her.

Imagine my further frustration when, after she offers a description of her young female relative that is unable to feed herself and more (indeed unfortunate), she asks whether Dawkins believes the young girl has a soul. She honestly feels that evolutionists and atheists don't have compassion for people that are physically or emotionally challenged. From where does she get her information? She is under the impression that, evolution and natural selection being a 'survival-of-the-fittest' kind of thing, that non-utilitarian people are going to be trampled on if evolutionists had their way. These people are investigating evolution by natural selection as it happens in nature! Where is the corollary thinking that these investigations translate into a PHILOSOPHY of living by these scientists? There IS no corollary. We DO live in a world where most people feel compassion towards others.

She is, yet again, misstating the facts. Evolutionists, biologists and atheists do not have a doctrine or a philosophy. For Pete's sake let's get this right people! Evolutionists (along with biologists and all the other scientists from the various disciplines that are involved in the study of the aforementioned) are simply studying the evidence FOR evolution and they (and everyone else) are testing and re-testing the results to see if they stand up. Atheists (as you would have learned by now) simply do not believe in any god's. WHAT PHILOSOPHY? I am still seething 2 years after this interview!

Another rather blatant 'duh' moment on her part comes when Professor Dawkins genuinely and thoughtfully explains that even HE would not want to be part of a purely Darwinian society (relating to the process of natural selection and its rather violent, 'survival-of-the-fittest reality'). This society would arguably be "*a ruthless, free-market economy in which the rich trampled the poor*", opposite of a liberal-socialist society where the wealthy would help the not so fortunate. "*The facts of science show the world of nature is a Darwinian world. It's a very unpleasant world. It's a thoroughly unpleasant world. NOT the kind of world we wish to live in, so let us understand it so that we can construct the kind of society in which we wish to live, which will be a NON-Darwinian society. It will be the sort of society that DEPARTS from Darwinian principles.*" He was obviously, again, giving an analogy to the cutthroat, survival-oriented nature of natural selection and applying that to a hypothetical society based on those principles. Ms. Wright showed her ignorance even further by saying that he had made HER point!

She begins from another angle "*Recognizing that there is a loving creator helps to build a society that is more than just livable, but pleasant,*" she states. So am I to interpret this to mean that even though god is a figment of the imagination of copper-age man that we all have to believe that there is not only a god that started it all but a loving one as well?? PLUS the fact that that belief is the only way we can have a happy society? If that is the general consensus out there I am truly embarrassed to be a part of the human race.

Say it ain't so.

Yet ANOTHER misunderstanding by Wendy Wright shines through. Ms. Wright seems to think that the 'evidence' that does NOT back-up evolution should be taught in the schools. She refers to this as "the controversies". She does not seem to be getting it at all. Yes, science IS about testing and re-testing hypotheses to see if they will stand up. However, if there WERE an element around evolution that does not stand up (that would suggest perhaps another alternative that seems reasonable) then we would know about it. It would have to be monumental, after all the theory of evolution has withstood all comers for 150 years. There are always going to be discussions about evidence-found where scientists are not sure where that piece fits in the overall scale of things and OF COURSE every fossil found will be a 'controversy', until it is proven (or disproven) to be helpful (or not) towards the evolutionary theory. Thousands of fragments of fossils are found every year, but I hope Ms. Wright is not going to suggest we start a whole series of books telling of all the fossils we are not sure about yet! Even though there are discussions about to what degree certain things like Genetic drift, natural selection and variation have on the evolutionary process, the Evolutionary theory is going to be around a very long time Wendy, better get used to it!

Of course there are frauds out there too but we DO try to discount them when they are revealed. To mention a Victorian-era mistake and then blame the scientific community for perpetuating THAT as one of the reasons FOR the evolutionary theory is just plain insulting. It's almost like blaming every human for having a useless appendix! (Well, I never said I was good at making analogies, lol). EVERY facet of life has it's fraudulent practitioners but I don't see how mentioning all those 'controversies' is going to help any.

That would take away from all the real tried-and-true facts of evolution. The truth that Ms. Wright has blinders on regarding the FACT of evolution is just sad, and her objections to it don't carry much weight with me. In this age of the Internet, if there was one major thing that was found to make evolution a bad theory, again, we would have heard about it. An overwhelming majority of scientists AND theologians ACCEPT the FACT of evolution. Considering she thinks there is an actual creator that "loves us out there somewhere" (the Judeo-Christian one, of course) well, *talk about a 'controversy' of epic proportions*

She then introduces a new discussion by saying that God has "*Intervention at the point of each person's creation.*" I am lost. So now god is present at the conception of each person.... Oh, K.. Here we come to the part about DNA. Ms. Right fervently believes that the DNA in each of us represents a uniqueness that shows that god creates each of us to be a special being. Dawkins rightly states that the whole CONCEPT of natural selection and evolution MUST work on the variants of individual 'uniqueness', otherwise evolution and selection would not work. Her example of a recessive gene (she cites a hypothetical male and female having 13 children and one has blue eyes where all the others have brown eyes) AGAIN is a misunderstanding of the science of it, and how it relates to natural selection. Contrary to her belief in the 'uniqueness' of that blue-eyed individual being created by god, it is a prime example of how the natural selection process is intended to work. If the blue-eyed feature was replaced by a unique disease or other impediment to that individuals survival compared to her 12 siblings, then she/he would perhaps not reproduce, thereby allowing the other 12 who were NOT impeded by that hypothetical disease to reproduce and survive. Sorry, Wendy. Ms. WRONG again.

The funny thing is, if Professor Dawkins had started to talk more about this subject and introduced, say, the recessive inherited trait of juvenile onset diabetes, I wonder what Ms Wright would have said? "*God works in mysterious ways*", I would imagine would be one of her possible responses. To be sure, the unfortunate recipient of those destructive, recessive traits usually die in childhood before passing it on to the next generation. This would have been a great example to Ms. Wright as to how natural selection works. This person would not have had children, thus slowly eliminating the possibility of this gene being passed down to even further generations and, more importantly with a 'nod' to the natural-selection process, allowing people WITHOUT that gene to multiply and survive. Natural selection at its finest. Nasty stuff though, to be sure. Natural selection takes no prisoners, but to ignore the science of it, and to attribute the individuality of our DNA to gods hand is fundamentalism, pure and simple.

When asked whether or not she agreed with critical-thinking being taught in the classroom, Ms. Wright seemed to agree. Her answer in the positive surprised me a bit, as her own obvious LACK of critical-thinking prevented her from stepping back a little from her fundamental position and to really take in some of the basics Dawkins offered. Evidence not recognized: a society based on Darwinian principles misinterpreted. And the list goes on.

To conclude, it is the sheer vastness of Wendy Wright's inflexibility that prompted me to write this bit about her. I am sure she is a hard-working, hard-nosed adversary against all who might cross her path and is otherwise mostly effective in her many causes. Unfortunately, as seen many times by people, blind faith gets in the way of common sense, reason, and a step back to 'look at the evidence'. One can only hope that Ms. Wright has taken another look at her talk with Professor Dawkins on that day, and squirms a little when she hears what she actually said. Just a little.

SCIENTISTS THAT DON'T BELIEVE IN EVOLUTION

As amazing as it seems, there are scientists that do not believe in evolution. It is interesting to note, however, that the majority of these have done what appears to be a total 'conversion', from rationally thinking individuals to devout believers in whatever faith seems to move them. These do not seem to be scientists that have looked at all the insurmountable evidence FOR evolution and made an attempt at offering an alternative. It's almost like they are scrambling in an attempt to show how they have 'seen the light', but, as you will see below, their arguments don't stand up to scrutiny. Here is an excerpt from a popular website called ASSOCIATED CONTENT (the peoples media company). This article is specifically about scientists that do not believe the theory of evolution. It mentions many of the scientists as being former 'believers' in the theory, only to have made a 180-degree 'about turn'. The following is a direct quote from the article and mentions 2 people:

One scientist, who once called himself an "atheistic evolutionist," but now is a Christian, is one such scientist. "*He says he once considered a good time for him was drinking beer with his friends and mocking Billy Graham on television. He also mocked the idea that people are sinners. He now teaches creation science workshops for a living.*" The article continues:

"*One teacher who doubts evolution points out that at one point scientists believed evolution could not be proven because the number of fossils to be observed was too few.*" He said "100 years later, despite the discovery of many more fossils, it has not been proven-because there is no example of a new species or one species turning into another." He also mentions "*models of evolution such as the Peking Man, the Piltdown Man, and the Nebraska Man have all been proven to be hoaxes but still appear in textbooks.*" "*All living creatures are divided into distinct types, and, if evolution were true, there should be many creatures that cannot be classified, but there are not. There are many examples of species becoming extinct, but not of new ones forming.*"

Point #1 "*The number of fossils to be observed was too few*". In Florissant Fossil Beds National Monument ALONE over 140 species of plants have been discovered, not to mention over 1,400 species of insects, and all this in just a 12 X 1-mile area. I could write a separate book about all the fossils discovered on earth, covering several volumes, although I doubt Ms. Wright would look at it.

Point #2 He said "*100 years later, despite the discovery of many more fossils, it has not been proven-because there is no example of a new species or one species turning into another.*" One basic point this so-called 'scientist' fails to understand is that a species does not just "turn into another. At least not overnight. The 'SPECIATION' (for example) part of the evolutionary process is how one species changes over time to the point where that population is distinct and can no longer interbreed with the "parent" population. In order for this new species to develop it is necessary for several populations of the same species to be separated somehow. Often times there is a physical boundary that keeps the same species apart for thousands (even millions) of years. If each population (of the same species) is exposed to different-enough environmental factors, they will develop differently. The 'reproductive isolation' of the populations (assuming the geographical distance between them is too great for continued inter-breeding) of this hypothetical organism will ensure that they will become distinct species, SEPARATE from the original 'parent' group. This is one example of how totally different species can develop.

Point #3 He also says that "*models of evolution such as the Peking Man, the Piltdown Man, and the Nebraska Man have all been proven to be hoaxes but still appear in textbooks.*" I have already mentioned that out-right frauds (when they are found out) are NOT used as evidence FOR evolution. In our relatively transparent society today, with everything on the Internet, and 100's of millions of people as an enormous 'peer' group ready to challenge ANYTHING, such frauds would hardly stand up today. To say they have already been proven to be hoaxes and are still in textbooks is either leaving out an important fact (that the mere MENTION of these in modern books suggests that they DO tell of their 'fraudulency') or suggesting that scientists, on the whole, are seriously trying to pull the wool over our eyes in the face of so much attention to this area of discussion by all of the computer-connected world. In the end, reason and critical-thinking will allow most of us to come to a reasonable conclusion about a lot of things. Believing in a divine, loving creator. Well.. SOME might say THAT has been the biggest hoax to have been perpetrated in all of human history! Mull THAT over a bit and see where it takes you.

Point #4 Next he states that "*all living creatures are divided into distinct types.*" He adds that "*if evolution were true, there should be many creatures that cannot be classified, but there are not.*" If one cares to look into the various types of taxonomic classifications of all living things, one realizes that it would be incredibly difficult NOT to be able to classify an organism into one group or another. There are also intermediate steps in the classification process, which makes the identification even more precise. To suggest this is a reason NOT to believe in the evolutionary theory is just ridiculous, even if it were true. And (if reason is going to play a part here in ANY form) it might be presumed (by a non-scientist who accepts evolution as fact) that if there ARE any organisms that cannot be classified (because of an anomaly of growth or other distinction) then perhaps, JUST PERHAPS, that might indicate an intermediary that is on its way TO becoming a distinct species. Put THAT in your collective theistic pipes and smoke them.

Point #5 He continues... "*There are many examples of species becoming extinct, but not of new ones forming*". As I stated above, most species come to be after splitting from an ancestral species when they acquire new adaptations to a changing environment and, over time, BECOME the species to which you are referring. AGAIN, if these scientists ever read an evolutionary book, they would realize that around 98 percent of species that have ever populated our planet have become extinct! Some of the millions of living species today would, I assume, be the 'NEW' species this scientist was talking about. What, exactly, is your point?

In conclusion, one can see that there are a lot of people that deny the evolutionary theory (for religious, personal or political reasons) and that every attempt to show the machinations of the concept simply falls on deaf ears.

Whether these religious stalwarts have bad science, incomplete ideas, misinterpretations of the facts or plain ignorance to make their point, the end result is a temporary roadblock for the atheist (I meant anti-theist) in attempting to enlighten the population, and to get them thinking for themselves

What a concept.

Chapter Seven

THE BIBLE, and some of it's shortcomings

When you consider that the present-day Judeo-Christian bible had been written over almost 1,500 years (1,400 BC to around 90 AD) with 66 separate books and has around 40 noted and widely-accepted authors to it's credit, it is easy to see how important the study of these documents are in order to get an idea of who we were. It is a part of our history.

You know I really DON'T have a bee-in-my-bonnet against the majority of the rank-and-file person who, benignly and passively, MAY have an inclination towards a religion of their choice. Many (as I have indicated in earlier chapters) don't really care one way or the other, as their lives are undoubtedly complicated enough to worry about such things. I don't get it, but I understand.

I am sure that is the way it is with most people. I have also mentioned that I am more concerned with what is real and truthful; what can be determined by a reasonable amount of data and evidence to support a claim/event-- whatever, than putting down the majority of people that simply have a community, historical, societal, traditional connection to this church or that synagogue.

Having said that, what we have left are hundreds of millions of people who really believe many of the stories of their chosen faith (according to a gallop poll almost one third of Americans), and a small percentage of THEM that carry out horrible actions against other people, based on a maniacal indoctrination in their faith. We also have a humongous religious infrastructure that continues to pound religious ideas into new generations, denying these children a comparative introduction to earth's various religions. We have touched on this subject in former chapters, far-be-it from me to beat a dead horse, and I will leave it there but with a final comment.

It has become apparent to me, writing this book that the most amazing thing about our major religions is that they continue to be practiced AT ALL today. It HAS to be patently obvious to any reasonably intelligent person that it has been simply the power, money, and political ties that have kept religion alive and well. THAT, and also the fact that for millennia its potential flock was predominantly uneducated, unsophisticated and unwise in the ways of the world, and was ripe for the picking. I don't want to go into a complex history of the bible. However, for the purpose of this book, it is prudent of me to look into the origins of the bible and how it all came together, as well as discuss the issue I have with the content of the bible, after all it's precepts, stories and rules are the basis for the Judeo-Christian faith, are they not?

One common explanation of the differences between the Old and New Testament is that the former explains the latter. Before I go on, here is an exact transcript of a statement by the good folks at http://WWW.GOTQUESTIONS.ORG, when asked what the differences are between the Old and New Testaments.

Answer: "*The Old Testament lays the foundation for the teachings and events found in the New Testament. The Bible is a progressive revelation. If you skip the first half of any good book and try to finish it, you will have a hard time understanding the characters, the plot, and the ending.*"

I tend to disagree with some of the wording in the transcript above when it gives a book as an analogy to the bible in that sense. A book is usually written with some kind of research and interest by the author, and is compiled within a reasonable time frame. It is ingenuous above all to say the modern bible is an original idea at all. The origins are lost forever. The original 'word of god' has been so much translated, transcribed, misinterpreted, re-organized and been done over several millennia YET THERE ARE STILL one third of Americans who believe the bible to be true! The present-day bible is only one way out of millions it could have turned out, due to the wide-ranging source material and limitless interpretations of the scribes who compiled it, etc. Amazing......

OF COURSE the Old Testament lays the foundation for the teachings and events found in the New Testament... I mean, how inconvenient were it not the case? It is only for the sheer power of the Christian church that prevented all and sundry from putting their own, unique spin on the New Testament and creating thousands of new branches of the Christian faith. As it stands there are 5 major traditional branches of Christianity today, and 18 major denominational families of Christianity, including Anglicans, Pentecostals and Quakers.

I can understand that any authors responsible for creating a book with the power to control huge groups of people would want to change the book to suit the times. However, it appears that the 'progression' of these books teachings, compiled over 1,500 years, came to a full stop before the 1st century was over. Is there nothing else God wants to do? Why did he seem to stop doing everything? Why do the stories stop there? One would think with all this rising from the dead, turning water into wine and all the rest that the show would go on for some time. After all, things like that do not happen every day, and if they were true, one would think that an encore would be appropriate....

I don't think it is out of place here to mention that it seems like (as we know the bible was compiled from oral and written sources from around 1,400 BC) there is much controversy over the actual age of the earth and when god actually did all his creating, at least from the theist camp. Another book could be written about this subject, but it seems that this 'dispute' falls along the same lines as one would expect. The Young Earth creationist theory of an earth less than 10,000 years old has held fast only because of devout belief and a fairly convenient interpretation of the bible. Radioisotopes and the Age of the Earth (R.A.T.E.) was formed by devout believers to try to debunk the current science of radioactive dating of rocks to determine the age of surrounding fossils, etc.. None of their findings have been peer-reviewed and it is said that they do not have enough experience in experimental geochronology--"*Geochronology is the science of determining the absolute age of rocks, fossils, and sediments, within a certain degree of uncertainty inherent to the method used*" (http://en.wikipedia.org/wiki/Geochronology).

One person that does not seem to be mentioned, and that I think needs to be, (might as well throw one bone to the theistic side) is Isaac Ben Samuel of Acre. He was a Kabbalist who lived in Israel around 1,200 AD.

and predicted the age of the earth to be around 15 billion years old. His theory was based on a verse from Psalms, which states "*A thousand years in your sight are but as yesterday*" (Psalm 90:4). "*If each day of a divine year was equal to a thousand earthly "solar years," then a divine year would be 365,250 years long. This does not differ so much from the scientific community's estimate on the age of the universe (currently at 13.75 billion years).*" I DO NOT include this as support for the scientific estimate, as his was clearly a non-scientific method (just an interpretation of a small psalm). I do find it interesting, though, that no one in the modern religious community seems to be promoting his estimate. For obvious reasons, I would think at least SOME theists would like to see a more 'coming-together' of the positions of science and religion, and this man's Kabbalic prediction would do that, in spades. Let's leave it at that.

I suppose I should not sound so cavalier about my position on the bible, but I am always amazed at why so many people believe in the stories and canons of the New Testament, when it is clearly a compilation meant for a truly ancient audience, largely uneducated. Living in the modern world, as we presently do, one would think a huge revolution would have happened before now, decrying the old, tired precepts of the two testaments and that we would have invented something else, perhaps a study more around the awe of science and how that is the best hope we have, as humans, to understand the world around us.

Interesting is what it is that we have all been worshiping these last 1,800 years or so. I can't even imagine how many translations there must have been over this period of time. Considering that Jesus spoke Aramaic, and there are no known surviving Aramaic texts, we don't even have the original words of god with which to translate! Also, consider that without the advances of the modern printing press, centuries of subjective translations from non-Aramaic texts, hand-written, would have had to be the ones relied on for subsequent generations.

Everyone knows about the books Matthew, Luke, Mark, and John, but I wonder how many people know that these are hardly the original writings? To understand how subjective and thrown-together these four famous canons are, consider this explanation of how these four came to be. This is a direct transcript written by noted biblical scholar, William M. Schniedewind from www.maplenet.net and it goes like this:

"Our four canonical gospels did not begin their lives as the gospels of "Matthew," "Mark," "Luke" and "John." Different groups of early Christians maintained their own oral traditions of Jesus' wisdom, as writing was a specialized skill and not every fellowship enjoyed the services of a scribe. When written accounts of Jesus' teachings began to circulate (i.e., the theoretical "sayings" gospel Q and the Semeia or Signs source), the independent groups would supplement them with their own traditions about the savior, each believing their own versions to be "the Gospel." Eventually, as these expanded writings spread through other communities, some versions were viewed as having more authority than others. It was not until the pronouncement of Bishop Irenus (185 C.E.) that Christians began to accept only the four familiar gospels as authoritative, and to refer to them by their modern titles."

Looks like a whole LOT of subjective story telling from many different bronze-age tribes went into making up the bible 'we' all pray about today. Still amazing to me.

It is easy to see how people believe what they want to believe (or are told to believe). I imagine that there are many differences between the original teachings of Jesus of Nazareth and what Christians read and believe today. What with 'writing being a specialized skill', any wonder what the average intelligence-level must have been of the poor suckers who bought into all this back then? After reading this chapter, I would think most people would agree that the bible that was written for ancient Middle-eastern Jews is not the same bible that we should honor today. At the very least, most people end up quoting the nice parts and reverse-cherry-pick out the bad. I am sure most devout theists would take every bad deed/statement I find in the bible and tell me that the particular psalm in question was an allegory, or that deed was an example to make one think about (whatever) an so on.....

Sorry, cherry-picking is not allowed. It is either your holy book or it is not. If the bible is supposed to be the inspired words of god then let it lay and deal with it. If your perfect and most omnipotent God can't speak to allow a concise book to be written, and to be interpreted, clearly by the very devotees and 'end-users' of his advice, then he clearly IS a figment of your imagination. The bible IS full of inconsistencies, and that would be consistent with man's attempt at a first draft of a book. Too many cooks spoil the broth.

When I bring these points up in discussions I am often taken-to-task by believers who question my authority on religious matters. "*Do I have a masters in theology*"?? Well, no.. Truth-be-told... I don't. However, since I have not been given any evidence to suggest that any god has ever existed (with the exception of in the mind of the believer) I hardly think it rational to educate myself in something that does not exist.... or, rather in something that is BASED on something that is not true. I can certainly educate myself enough in the general idea of the world's religions to make sense of my chosen topic for this book.

The bible took a long time to spring into existence. Long before the written word was available to even royalty or the high priests, oral teachings were the way of things. Eventually, writing in some form was adopted by, of course, the ruling class and their religious friends, who controlled and manipulated writing to their own tastes. As usual, writing was seen as being some kind of 'gift from the gods', and was protected as such.

Biblical literature flourished and from the 8th to the 6th century BC a lot of this writing took place. As the economies of ancient Palestine and Jerusalem grew, writing became an all-important function of the time.

From PBS.org (2008)--- "*At the end of the eighth century in both Mesopotamia and Egypt, rulers were collecting the ancient books (scrolls), and ancient Judeans followed their model, collecting the traditions, stories, and laws of their ancestors into written manuscripts.*"

Keep in mind that the bible (as we know it today) was not around at that time. In fact, there were no books around then. It was only near the first century A.D. that codices (bound leaves of paper resembling today's books) were used by Christianity, even though other religions asserted the authority of the living voice of the teacher, rather than the printed word. By this time the teachings, both oral and written, were compiled into what we now know as the Old and New Testaments.

I give you this brief summary of how the bible was created to illustrate how interesting and challenging it must have been for the religious scholars of that era to compile these books into the two testaments that live on to this day. It also shows that, far from being a book that was created in a relatively short time, with god's word and his miracles and all, it was created 'hodgepodge' over 1,500 years by nomadic tribes, exiled communities and the religious elite with political control. Any wonder I have a hard time wondering how anyone can dedicate themselves to a holy book that was conjured up from all sorts of sources over a huge expanse of time? That's all these are... stories.

Any objective listener and viewer of these events would have to say that the bible was, indeed, one of our first attempts to write a cohesive collection of our thoughts down, spanning a lot of time. I personally think that this is a great achievement. Our first book. Cool. It took a long time to get going, but since the religious folks were in charge, it was unlikely that a cookbook would have been the first great triumphant literary accomplishment. I must continue to throw up my hands and wonder why we still continue to believe in a book that was the first one written. Even if you claim worshipping a man-made god gives you comfort, one would think that a bible (perhaps a scientific Bible?) written more near the 20th century would make more sense for today's people, don't you?

We could ALL take some comfort from that.

Chapter Eight

THE BIBLE-- IS IT MORALLY CORRUPT?

This chapter is going to be revealing in one major way. The old and new testaments of the bible stand as they have always. There are those that will choose the good parts and say the bible is all about the positive stories, but the bible is FULL of dark, negative dealings that happened to be a part of life, I suppose, back in ancient Palestine and surrounding areas. Of course there is not a theologian alive today who wants to kill someone who changes his or her religion. No one wants to go into town and murder people because a few folks decided to worship a golden calf. Nobody wants to revel in the really awful parts of the bible, and the really GOOD parts are going to be lauded over us. Of course we have all grown up and realized that a lot of the bible does not apply to today's general moral ways.

However, that does not let the bible and it's proponents off the hook. The bible is, for better or worse, the only thing binding the Christian faith together. The very precepts of the bible have been followed for over 2 thousand years, and today's Fundamentalists are quite confident in their literal interpretation. In this chapter, I will show you some of the primitive, backwards and utterly despotic verses contained within the bible, further mystifying me how this religion (and others like it) can continue to be promoted by the religious community today.

There are many incongruence's, fallacies and historical untruths that fill the Judeo-Christian bible. One that comes to mind is an important prophetical statement in the bible that says that Jesus was born in the house of David. That means Bethlehem. Jesus of Nazareth is commonly known to have been born (guess where?)......in Nazareth! It has been found that NONE of the story of the Nativity is true. The falsehoods that had to be perpetrated in the bible to get Jesus of Nazareth to Bethlehem are evident by anyone taking the time to read into these things.

Before we continue it is worth noting that God, as the perfect, omnipotent being he is, would not have allowed any inconsistencies in his bible, since the book is supposed to be the inspired word of him/her...In fact, if he is so perfect then one would think that he would have sent down to earth a beautifully bound bible with EXACTLY the correct stories. No interpretation necessary. Read the following and you will begin to see this is not the case. The only conclusion that can be made by any rational being is that the word of the bible is only the word of man, full of inconsistencies that one would expect from a book cobbled together over 1,500 years by imperfect beings.

At the time of the nativity, a census was supposed to have taken place, with Joseph returning to his own town of David (Bethlehem) to be counted in this 'world census'. According to James Douglas Grant Dunn, Jesus Remembered, p. 344; E. P. Sanders, The Historical Figure of Jesus, Penguin, 1993, p86 we get the following quote: "*No historical sources mention a worldwide or even a Roman-controlled world census which would cover the population as a whole; those of Augustus covered Roman citizens only, and it was not the practice in Roman censuses to require people to return to their ancestral homes.*"

Furthermore, no agreement can be had between the four books of the New Testament on who the Governor was at the time Jesus was born, nor on the actual date of Christ's birth!! Do some research into the time of King Herod and see for yourselves the great deceptions that go into creating the stories of the bible. One never knows where historical fact begins and quaint story-telling ends.

There are just too many inconsistencies and contradictions in the bible for me to include them in this chapter. Indeed, one could write a complete book just listing them. I will be true to this chapter, however, and give you a few for you to 'enjoy'. Here it goes:

1 Genesis 1:3-5 (King James Version)

3 And God said, "*Let there be light": and there was light.*

4 *And God saw the light, that it was good: and God divided the light from the darkness.*

5 *And God called the light Day, and the darkness he called Night. And the evening and the morning were the first day.*

However, in Genesis 1:14-19 we have 19-"*And the evening and the morning were the fourth day.*" Which is it, the first day or the fourth? One would think that was pretty important, especially if that Kabbalist above was correct in his 'age of the earth' calculation.....

2) This next one has to do with god wanting us to procreate, but, in an about-face penalizes the woman for having a child. Not only that, poor animals have to be given as burnt offerings to the lord!!! In Genesis 1:28 we get the following: 28:-"*And God blessed them, and God said unto them, Be fruitful, and multiply, and replenish the earth, and subdue it: and have dominion over the fish of the sea, and over the fowl of the air, and over every living thing that moveth upon the earth.*"

Leviticus 12:1-8 paraphrases--" *If a woman have conceived seed, and born a man child: then she shall be unclean seven days; and she shall continue in the blood of her purifying threescore and six days.*" "*And if she be not able to bring a lamb, then she shall bring two turtles, or two young pigeons; the one for the burnt offering, and the other for a sin offering: and the priest shall make an atonement for her, and she shall be clean.*" sounds to me like it would have been easier to adopt......

Too many more to list here, so let's move on to the meatier stuff, shall we?

How about questionable moral values? Well, I am sad to say the bible is full of them.

From Deuteronomy 14,21 we get..... "*Ye shall not eat of anything that dieth of itself: thou shalt give it unto the stranger that is in thy gates, that he may eat it; or thou mayest sell it unto an alien.*"

Now, let me get this straight. If an animal dies of a disease, it is perfectly Christian of you not to eat the flesh yourself, but to make this diseased flesh available to any stranger you might meet, or to sell it at market, so that some family might benefit from it somehow. OUTRAGEOUS!

This is not an isolated part of the bible. I am not cherry-picking for my own purposes. I submit to you that ANY objective analysis of the bible will reveal a very dated, ancient-thinking, primitive collection of stories that can hardly base their validity on facts or morality, for that matter. Any GOOD parts of the bible (perhaps we can include the 10 commandments here... at least some of them) have been included as a result of secular behavioral truths, and nothing at all to do with an omnipotent god.

What about stealing from someone? Ahh, says the bible.."*THOU SHALT NOT STEAL*". OK, A noble thing to say. I am sure every theologian would pat himself or herself on the back supporting this. Then there's a bit more information garnered from the bible. Check out these two biblical statements. Not only do they seem to condone stealing, but in the worst way... under the guise of borrowing!! Here is EXODUS, the third chapter.... "*And I will give this people favor in the sight of the Egyptians: and it shall come to pass, that, when ye go, ye shall not go empty: but every woman shall borrow of her neighbor. And of her that sojourneth in the house, jewels of silver, and jewels of gold, and raiment: and ye shall put them upon your sons, and upon your daughters; and ye shall spoil the Egyptians.*" Nice going. In the twelfth chapter we get more eye-opening details... "*And the children of Israel did according to the word of Moses; and they borrowed of the Egyptians jewels of silver, and jewels of gold, and raiment: And the Lord gave the people favor in the sight of the Egyptians, so that they lent unto them such things as they required. And they spoiled the Egyptians.*" The bible seems to place this kind of thievery as an alright thing to do, as long as it is done on behalf of the lord. It turns out that it was the everyday Egyptian resident that would have been robbed in these cases, NOT the pharaohs who were the true despotic leaders of the day. It seems that the Judeo-Christian god had no other alternatives for reparations the Jews of the time were entitled to, after their suffering at the hands of the pharaohs. Some moral base THAT turned out to be.

A quite disturbing look into the bibles actual moral outlook can be obtained by looking at King James NUMBERS chapter 31. You don't have to be a biblical expert to read what happened here. The Lord said (and I paraphrase) "*Wipe out the Midians, take all the spoils for yourselves INCLUDING the women who had not slept with any of the Midian men (all the men and the women who HAD carnal relations with the men were executed) and Moses and the lord got a cut for themselves*!! Do all you theists understand this or is your blind faith allowing you to glaze over these blatant facts?

Slavery. Here we go again. We all know how degrading the concept of slavery is. Humans have used it ever since control was desired over a particular group of people, and they were powerless to do anything about it. NO freedom. No liberty. No possibility to make one's own way in life. Slavery has been around since man has been around. In ancient Rome, before

Christianity showed up, the slave's situation was actually improving somewhat. The practice of Manumission of slaves (releasing them from service) was done quite a lot, more often because they were outliving their usefulness, or their jobs were no longer required. At any rate, this system gave them a chance to become productive members of society. Then came Christianity. For two thousand years serfdom and slavery has been common and one only has to go back in time a little bit to remind ourselves of our own history regarding slavery.

We expect the Bible (at least theists would have us believe so) to give us chapter-and-verse on how vehement it is to enslave people. This would go hand-in-hand with their 'objective moral base' theists often refer to. Well, let me give one and all a little bit of an education as to what the bible actually says. REMEMBER, the bible is a book that is a compilation of interpretations and stories from a long time ago, so I don't discount that these were the true feelings of the day. Hardly a text to follow for creating a moral existence though, but.....

Here is the twenty-first chapter of EXODUS: "*If thou buy an Hebrew servant, six years he shall serve; and in the seventh he shall go out free for nothing. If he came in by himself, he shall go out by himself; if he were married, then his wife shall go with him. If his master have given him a wife, and she have born him sons or daughters, the wife and her children shall be her master's, and he shall go out by himself. And if the servant shall plainly say, I love my master, my wife, and my children; I will not go out free: Then his master shall bring him unto the judges; he shall also bring him to the door, or unto the door post; and his master shall bore his ear through with an awl, and he shall serve him forever.*" So not only does the bible recognize slavery but it has a plan for the slave as well. The slave can leave after 6 years of service, but leave everything behind when he goes. He can leave with a wife, but ONLY if he came with a wife in the first place. If he married while in service to his master, and did not want to leave her and his children after the 6 years were up, he was forced to have an awl rammed into his ear!

Since we're talking about slavery, what about the bible allowing the master to kill his slave without punishment, as the slave is merely the masters 'money'. You won't believe this one, again in the twenty-first chapter, and here it goes: "*If a man smite his servant or his maid with a rod, and he die under his hand, he shall be surely punished. Notwithstanding, if he continue a day or two, he shall not be punished; for he is his money.*" Only when the slave falls dead beneath the blow shall the master be punished. But let the blow be equally fatal, let the man or the woman linger in agony and die the next day, and the murderous master must not be punished." If the poor servant dies right away, then sure, punish the master, but if the servant dies in agony a couple of days later then, pfft!, he is just the chattel of the master.... so be it. Those were harsh days indeed.

To continue with this theme, I also submit the following two New Testament statements, the first from Ephesians 6:5, which demonstrates the bibles acceptance of shackles and chains with respect to bondage of the slaves, and the second, from Timothy 6:1, Paul writes that the master should be worshipped as is Christ..... Here they are: 1) "*Servants, be obedient to them that are your masters according to the flesh, with fear and trembling, in singleness of your heart, as unto Christ*," and 2) "*Let as many servants as are under the yoke count their own masters worthy of all honor, that the name of God and his doctrine be not blasphemed.*" I mean really, I am not making this stuff up. This is the bible speaking here. This is an ancient peoples writings, as they undoubtedly thought and felt in their day and time. I'm not blaming them for having these common thoughts as they were, but it is hardly acceptable stuff for the betterment of mankind. Secularists have done a far better job.

As this chapter is about the inconsistencies and the barbaric nature of the writings on many of the books of the new and old testaments, I shall continue.

From the thirteenth chapter of Deuteronomy we see that Christianity is okay with killing someone if they decide to go to another religion. Again, I am not making this up: "If thy brother, the son of thy mother, or thy son, or thy daughter, or the wife of thy bosom, or thy friend, which is as thine own soul, entice thee secretly, saying, 'Let as go and serve other gods.' Thou shalt not consent unto him, nor hearken unto him, neither shalt thine eye pity him, neither shalt thou spare, neither shalt thou conceal him. But thou shalt surely kill him; thine hand shall be first upon him to put him to death, and afterwards the hand of all the people. And thou shalt stone him with stones that he die." I don't think this statement needs any further deliberation. Talk about control of the masses.

Deuteronomy must have cornered the market on diabolical actions towards the human race, and it continues in chapter 17.... "If there be found among you within any of thy gates . . . man or woman that hath . . . gone and served other gods and worshipped them, either the sun, or moon, or any of the host of heaven . . . Then shalt thou bring forth that man or that woman, which have committed that wicked thing unto thy gates and thou shalt stone them with stones till they die." The sheer wonderment of the universe around us (the awe-inspiring natural world the atheist sees WITHOUT the need for a supreme being) has been formally decried in this verse. Sun worship, perhaps the oldest and most natural of 'religions,' is surely a death-sentence to the doer, according to biblical terms.

The New Testament is no better at dealing with religious progression than the old. In Galatians 1:9, Paul says: "If any man preach any other gospel unto you than that ye have received, let him be accursed." Well, if that was not harsh enough, try this one from Jesus himself, From LUKE 19:27 "But those mine enemies, which would not that I should reign over them, bring hither, and slay them before me." AND IF YOU ARE NOT STILL CONVINCED, this one is from the last chapter of the gospel of Mark, "He that believeth and is baptized shall be saved; but he that believeth not shall be damned."

Not that I really want to go there, but a look into the acceptance of cannibalism should not be overlooked when listing the bibles most infamous texts. AGAIN, the 28th chapter of Deuteronomy states that: "And thou shalt eat the fruit of thine own body, the flesh of thy sons and of thy daughters, which the Lord thy God hath given thee. . . The man that is tender among you shall eat "the flesh of his children . . . The tender and delicate woman among you ... her eye shall be evil toward her children which she shall bear: for she shall eat them." Disgusting. From the ninth verse of the nineteenth chapter of Jeremiah we get: "And I will cause them to eat the flesh of their sons, and the flesh of their daughters, and they shall eat every one the flesh of his friend." 'INSPIRED' words, perhaps, but one can't escape the possibility that these verses were the work of madmen.

The story goes that some people had been found out to have been worshipping a golden calf. To punish them, and to show how religion was meant to control the masses, we get this statement from the thirty-second chapter of EXODUS, and it goes like this: "Thus saith the Lord God of Israel, put every man his sword by his side, and go in and out from gate to gate throughout the camp, and slay every man his brother, and every man his companion, and every man his neighbor." I suppose murder was an accepted religious practice, then? Here is yet another order from god, as stated in the fifteenth chapter of I Samuel: "Now go and smite Amalek, and utterly destroy all that they have, and spare them not; but slay both man and woman, infant and suckling, ox and sheep, camel and ass." Kill the men, women and infants and, while you're at it, wipe out the animals too.

The famous (or infamous) Joshua was said to be protected by god, and so he set out to conquer the 'promised land'... here is the act in a nutshell, from the tenth chapter of the book of Joshua: "So Joshua smote all the country of the hills, and of the south, and of the vale, and of the springs, and all their kings: he left none remaining, but utterly destroyed all that breathed, as the Lord God of Israel commanded." Whole lotta 'smotin' goin' on.

I think I have given reasonable, but by no means exhaustive, examples of the negative, amoral ideas put forth in the two testaments. "The Bible says, "Thou shalt not kill," and then proceeds to recite a long and gruesome catalogue of murders, massacres and wars of conquest for which it claims the approval or command of God. Hence the Bible is a dangerous moral guide." the bible says, "thou shalt not steal", and then, as if behind the scenes, gives a thumbs-up to the follower of god to commit all kinds of thievery in his name.

Here are some more, if the ones already posted were not enough:

1) From ROMANS, chapter 13- "Let every soul be subject unto the

higher powers. For there is no power but of God: the powers that be are ordained of God. Whosoever therefore resisteth the power, resisteth the ordinance of God: and they that resist shall receive to themselves damnation." Wicked words indeed...

2) "Then God said, "Take your son, your only son Isaac, whom you love, and go to the region of Moriah. Sacrifice him there as a burnt offering on one of the mountains I will tell you about." (Genesis 22:2) Now, God supposedly intervened just before Abraham was about to make a bonfire out of his son, but Abraham was willing to do it to show his allegiance to this God. How utterly devastating for the human race; willing to accept such a controlling master.

3) And Jephtah made a vow to the Lord, and said "If you will give the Ammonites into my hand, then whoever comes out of the doors of my house to meet me, when I return victorious from the Ammonites, shall be the Lord's, to be offered up by me as a burnt offering". Judges 11:29-33 The story goes that his only daughter ran out of his house to greet him upon returning from his victorious battle, and she was, umm, toast. From www.womeninthebible.net we get- "In later times, the Israelites were horrified by the idea of human sacrifice and had strict teachings against it. However, it may have existed in the early period of Jewish history." Horrified by the idea of human sacrifice. SEE? I TOLD you humans have the power of learning and the ability to move forward! The problem here is that you cannot escape what WAS written, and I will not condone cherry-picking to justify the bible as something that should be followed. Wake up and realize that you ARE following an ancient religion, prepared for ancient people. Try fishing or learning a musical instrument or something. Much more satisfying.

4) "let seven men of his sons be delivered unto us, and we will hang them up unto Jehovah in Gibeah of Saul, the chosen of Jehovah. And the king said, I will give them." This was the price these seven had to pay for an attack on the Gibeonites, to appease god and to "bless the inheritance of Jehovah. ⅃ Cruel and unusual punishment, I would say.

5) EXODUS - chapter twenty-two, "Thou shalt not suffer a witch to live," A religious OKAY to kill any person (usually a woman) for the ridiculous charge of being a witch. We all know how THAT turned out.

To conclude, as inspired and as holy a book as the bible is claimed to be, it certainly seems to be giving the go-ahead to commit all kinds of sadistic, cruel and unusually provocative acts against one another, all in the name of God. If this was how it actually was back then, and we know that the world was at constant war all the time, then I am actually glad we have this quasi-historical reference to those awful days. If anything, it shows us the extent to which people were expected to behave as a devotee of the almighty. Thanks to reason, we have allowed the bar to be raised, morally-speaking. To most of us, it has... as for the rest, we are all aware of the potential carnage when a religiously guided zealot goes crazy.

As for me, I've about had it with this eye-opening but depressing look at the world's most popular holy book. It surely is to our credit that we don't sacrifice our first-born anymore!

On to other topics.....

CHAPTER Nine

Who 'created' the Coca Cola can?

How was the universe created, and how did we come to be here? Wow! Two questions for the ages. Are we ever really going to find out the answer to the first one? The second one is well on it's way to being answered but I would like to spend this chapter on the former, going over some of the ideas being bantered around by the sage minds of our world.

The very notion of what (or who) created the laws of nature and our universe has had many proponents of faith coming out with several ideas. Actually, they seem to pose more questions than answers (at least any with a reasonable hypothesis) and what you hear leaves the Evolutionists cold and scratching their collective heads. Not to say that the complex theories of science, too, leave the non-scientist with a gaping mouth, but at least they are attempting to unravel the mysteries, one piece of evidence at a time. One point I would like to make before we get going, is that I notice the more we talk about these origins the more the faith-based side tends to take the position that "science is not prepared to answer that". When asked: "How did the laws of nature (gravity, inertia, quantum mechanics, etc.) come into being", or "Is there an intelligent power behind it all?" The theologians are only too quick to point out that these questions are beyond the scope of science and can only be discussed in the realms of philosophy and metaphysics. Sorry, but that seems like a cop-out to me. Sure, it may be impossible NOW to know these answers, but how can anyone deny the amazing advances in the sciences and technology fields in the last 150 years? I will be using the same point throughout this book, as I reiterate AGAIN that just because science can't handle ALL the proof you need, I suggest it is a far better alternative to learn the TRUTH about all the advances in the various disciplines and how they each contribute to the evolutionary world than to simply raise your hands and wipe them off and state that 'god did it all'.. NOT GOOD ENOUGH.

Shoving the tough questions aside for the philosophers and Metaphysicists might be a great career move for THOSE folks, but it hardly addresses a solution for the perhaps 'do-able' questions, such as working on evolution and the inter-connectivity between a lot of life on this planet, as scientists are now doing. OK, getting back to the issue-at-hand. The following will be some theories (if you can call them that) by the theistic side that attempt to propose ideas as to how the universe and the always-constant laws of nature came to be.

These are some ideas stated by Donald l. Hamilton, seminary Professor of Biblical Preaching at Columbia International University, and sometimes I paraphrase to keep the ball rolling. Right off the bat he postulates from his book THE MIND OF MANKIND that "God is not a king who sits up on some faraway throne directing the actions of the universe. "God" is an Infinite Creative Power who created the 'Laws of Nature' and thereby brought the universe into existence." He suggests that god does not run everything, the laws of nature do. I would agree that the laws run everything, as we know them, but I would obviously stop short and deny that a god created the laws, as he purports. Pretty heady stuff, to be sure. However he starts sidetracking right away and says that we all are not talking about the same god! One god, he states, "created the laws of inertia, gravity, energy, mass, etc." This is the one he says the secular folks talk about, supposedly, while the OTHER god is responsible for the "stories and commandments of religion". I mean, we can't even agree on which god we are all speaking about? Talk about a shell game!

He always emphasizes god is not responsible for all matter of things. He explains that when atheists ask him why bad things happen on earth if there is a god, (and this is a big one, PAY ATTENTION!) It is the "'Laws of Nature' NOT GOD! that runs the universe. Everything that happens is a consequence of these Laws - come what may. Besides - what is good for God does not necessarily have to be good for people. We live on a tiny speck of space dust in a universe of trillions of stars. God has his own priorities and we here on Earth are just an extremely minor part of his realm." WOW AGAIN!!! How, exactly did this guy ever get the job at the university?? Is he saying that god just threw our planet in with all the other stuff and let us fend for ourselves?? If we are so tiny and insignificant and he has better things to do than to mind us, maybe his statement is about as good as any for the Theory of Evolution and natural occurrence! Remind me to write that one down. Just when I was under the impression that we were the ultimate creation for him here on earth, I have been sorely mistaken. Uhhh. Which god were we talking about again??? Maybe I should debate this guy. He would end up making most of my points!

I don't know from which bible Professor Hamilton preaches and teaches, but I must tip my hat to him for yet ANOTHER of his statements, also from his book, that seems to say what all atheists say. "Religions are simply the outgrowth of ancient myths and dogmas handed down from generation to generation and formalized into faiths, rituals and tradition". I mean, well... YEAH!! I don't think I could have said it any better myself! You are the first theist I know that actually admits that religion is man-made, and therefore, by very definition, everything IN it is by man himself,

INCLUDING the statement that the bible "is the word of god". Unless I'm getting the wrong-end-of-the-stick, I think he would be better off arguing from the non-theist side of the table, don't you? Enough of THIS guy for a while, we may come back to him later in subsequent chapters. So much for that, Mr. Hamilton. You have not disappointed me yet!

Let's break for a minute and mention something interesting that seems to be possibly detrimental to the theist side of things, 'fundamentally-speaking'.

There is a rather new school of thought that is contending that there may be several 'middle-of-the-road' rationales on the beginnings of our universe. This one suggests that the book of Genesis (which most fundamentalists take as being literal) was written only in response to several regions around Bronze-age middle-east that had their OWN set of 'what-ifs?' The Mesopotamian and Egyptian people had their own deities in action, and some of their ideas conflicted.

Both these empires had deities and they were, for the most part, good AND evil, whereas the Hebrew god was only good (go figure). As well, these other places said the causes of creation were ACCIDENTAL as opposed to intentional. It might be also interesting to know that their deities were only finite in their sovereignty, as witnessed by the fact that Egypt was an amalgam of upper and lower states, so that many different deities came together in one big, super-natural mixer. The other reason for the rather short-lived rule of the worshipped was that the Ancient Egyptian civilization lasted for almost 3,000 years, and as society progressed, so did ideas, education and cultural values. In other words they 'grew out of their gods'. More or less.

The same school of thought is correctly stating that allegory was primarily used as the main teaching source, as the Ancient Hebrew system of education was virtually non-existent. That alone would normally be too trivial for me to include it in this chapter, were it not for the fact that they are saying that it is incredibly difficult to understand the intentional meaning of the original author(s) of the worlds holy books. Could that possibly mean that we CANNOT determine what (or who) created the universe by studying the bible? That intended viewpoint would have to have been first garnered from dozens of generations worth of stories and myths recorded down as text or drawings, or other object of communication. Then the 'extracted' meaning would have to be interpreted CORRECTLY by the reader. This seems to possibly be a 'bone-of-contention' for all the fundamentalists out there and, in this writers opinion, is just a bump-in-the-road (for the theists) on our way to proving the naturalistic viewpoint. (I would HATE to be the theist chosen to bring THIS stuff up at the next televised show!). At any rate, man wrote all these ancient books so we are back at the start again.

And now 'the Main event'! Just kidding. Like the previous Wendy Wright, it's not my style to single out any one person and fault them for a specific reason. I am finding it very hard, though, to ignore an impassioned argument from the 'Coca Cola Guy'. Here's one for the record books. No matter how many times I watch this I simply feel sorry for this person. Here he is, a man facing an audience of millions on National television, CONVINCED that he is about to tell all that he can PROVE gods ⸢ existence, 100% ⸢ and scientifically to boot! On his side is a famous young actor, Kirk Cameron, formerly of the television show GROWING PAINS (?) Well, the man's name is Ray Comfort and he is a Christian Minister, Evangelist and author. Now, I am not going to start bashing the poor guy.

Just go to YouTube and you will probably come to the conclusion that he may be somewhere, cowering in the shadows in the embarrassing aftermath of a televised debate that took place in 2007 on the ABC network. There were other separate programs involving a banana, but we will leave THAT story for the next chapter!!!

Here's the gist of the whole thing. The man gets on stage and holds up a Coke can. He says that the big bang caused rocks to form all over the place and on one of the rocks there was a brown, bubbly substance. Over millions of years, aluminum crept up the side of the can, creating the sides, top and the tab. Millions of years later red and white paint settled on the can and formed themselves into the words 'Coca Cola', etc. He rightly suggests that he is 'insulting our intelligence' by suggesting this. He goes on to say, "if you know the Coca Cola can was made, then there must be a maker". "'Where it's designed, there must be a designer", he states, referring to god's creation of the universe. "To believe this happened by sheer chance is to move into an intellectual-free zone", he sarcastically finishes. The design argument again.

He then proceeds to hold up a copy of the Mona Lisa and says that a hypothetical 12 scientists could come into the room and verify that it is, indeed, a painting and that it must have been painted. This statement was supposed to uphold his true-to-science methods by having had his (scientific) theories verified by experts in the field. Believe it or not, he does not stop there. Just in case the 4 million or more people watching didn't get the point by now, he starts talking about the building they are in using the same analogous form, as well as the new car he has that supposedly was put together over millions of years in his backyard!

Again, this argument is ancient and well known, NOT something that he miraculously came up with, and appears as various forms throughout history. There are 6 common forms, too deep to mention them here. He is basically using a Teleological argument. From philosophyonline.co.uk we get the summary "It is also known as the design argument and is based upon examination of the nature of the world. The main thrust of the argument is therefore that the world is too complex and well ordered to have been produced by chance or random change. This being so, it is argued that God is the only being responsible."

The main detrimental point of this argument is what the theologians call 'specified complexity'. Easy enough to understand. Simply, what we find in nature is 'similar' to what we know to have been designed. Both seem to be ordered and both seem to be fairly complex, therefore if one is designed, so is the other. That is a great leap and, as I said, the theistic side tanks again on this one in my humble opinion.

Talk about 'Growing Pains'.

It is well worth pointing out again here, at the risk of sounding repetitive, that no-one knows how the universe began IF, in fact, the universe ever had a start.

Make note of something here that may be of relevance to what we are discussing. The BIG BANG Theory. Everyone has heard of it. However were you aware that this theory does NOT, and I repeat, NOT claim to give an explanation of the 'creation' (for want of a better word) of the universe. Nor does it attempt to theorize what came before this event or what lies outside of the known universe. Theists are quite reasonably concerned with that. Not a competing theory to ultimate super-natural creation guys. Sorry.

No. What the theory DOES try to explain is how the universe developed from a very small, dense state into what we see in the observable universe today. The theory addresses the expansion of the universe. This means everything contained within space is spreading apart from everything else. It is theorized that the universe was extremely dense and at zero volume (actually called a 'singularity' in tech. terms). The universe expanded rapidly and thus cooled and became less dense. If it did not then, matter, as we know it, could not have formed. As radiation began to lose energy and matter began to form (naturally, I might add) we would have seen the universe with all its spinning systems moving away from each other as a result of their forward momentum and the forces of gravity, etc. I will mention now that there is a 100% consensus amongst scientists that the universe is actually expanding at a faster rate than previously thought. Unfortunately, it means that the entire Andromeda galaxy will be exterminating us in roughly 5 billion years. At least I have time for a few more rounds of golf (some design, god. Thanks a lot).

To be fair, the theory stated above, although inarguably the most famous and reasonably well thought-of, is by far NOT the only theory going. When you have the brightest minds of our planet working on the problem would not one expect just that? There are also theories-within-the-theory, which suggest the so-called "BIG BANG was not the beginning of the universe, just one of the many events like it", stated Paul Steinhardt of Princeton University. He continues by indicating that it is possible for the 'BANG' to have been a large collision between two universes where each existed in their own dimension, something that "happens every trillion years". One can see why theistic groups around the world would simultaneously implode if this were so. This part of the theory would seem to show that time has ALWAYS existed and will continue to exist. Well, I guess the idea of a creation event OR a creator would quickly die out in that case! This addition to the BIG-BANG theory can be related closely to the Steady State and Continuous Creation theory. Both have been thought not to be perfect, as the C.C.T. presumes instantly appearing hydrogen atoms that appear out of no-where and form galaxies to replace the ones that had previously been there to 'fill-the-gaps', as it were and allow the universe to look pretty-much the same forever (hence the name of Steady-State). Unfortunately this violates the Laws of Nature, as we know them. True, these laws are the ones we have now, but the statements of all these laws will have to be altered in deference to the way scientific theories are handled by experimental data, refutation and peer-review.

Another popular one is the Pulsating Universe Theory. As it's name implies, it is the expansion and contraction of the universe due to enormous gravitational pull. The present universe is expanding, but the gravitational pull will stop this and it will be contracted until more massive explosions occur, thereby expanding it again.

Suffice-it-to-say that it is, indeed, a very complex undertaking to be able to understand all the theories and ideas coming from the scientific world. 'Super-String theories' which needs space-time to have 11 dimensions! I have done some reading on these and I almost feel as though I am no further along that when I started! This is NOT a scientific book, so I will leave the above ideas with you. If you would like to investigate them further, then be my guest!

Whatever happened to the universe way back then (if anything happened to it at all) may never be found out. Speculation, proven and unproven theories might be with us for centuries and more. It is a shame that we DON'T have a titanium-clad, proof-and-evidence-filled explanation of the origins of our universe, as theists will be still uttering their familiar chants until they do. It is quite clear that it is science that is going to come close at getting the answer.

Meanwhile, we will continue to debate with creationists and proponents of intelligent design of the universe, over the existence of god and the theory of evolution by natural selection.

Chapter Ten

A look at some arguments from the theistic side and the rebuttals

This second chapter of three scattered in this book will focus on the more complex so-called 'logical' arguments theists have for the existence of God. In the following chapters we will look at more interesting themes see what questions theists have for us.. and we'll try to answer them.

Intelligent design (a 'designer' created the universe).

This is a so-called theistic 'scientific theory' that bases its main thesis on the 'irreducible complexity' of nature. In basic terms, life is far too complex to have started from simple beginnings, so it had to have been designed. It must be stated that this is NOT a theory (scientific, anyways), as it has no way of being tested. William Dembski's book 'The Design Inference', gives us only MORE water-muddying information, and suggests that "the principal characteristic of intelligent causation is directed contingency, or what we call choice." He continues.. "If the choice made is unlikely to occur and sufficiently complex, then we can attribute that choice to design. This comes from our understanding of how intelligent agents operate" What choices, then, did the thing that created the DESIGNER have to contend with when CREATING THE DESIGNER? The mind boggles.

Probably the most important theistic argument on the creation of the universe is the Teleological argument from William Paley, an 18th century theologian and philosopher. I mentioned it before but this is a more detailed look. As intriguing as this argument may seem from the initial glance, a simple analysis of it quite easily tears it apart. This is the basic argument and its axioms:

1) Everything we have seen that looks designed, has a designer.

2) The universe looks like it has been designed

3) Therefore the universe has a designer

4) The designer is god.

Most people that are aware of this argument have heard of the watch as being an analogous replacement for the universe. Assume that you happened to find a watch on the ground. You found the back missing and saw all the complex mechanisms that made up the inner workings of the timepiece. Automatically one would assume that it had been designed, right? It could not have appeared by accident. The human eye and brain are also complicated and therefore one might assume a creator was involved here as well. God MUST have created the universe then.

The stretch in this line of reasoning has a big flaw in logic, as I shall show. Since the whole point of this argument is to prove that everything has a designer, the first point above ASSUMES 'everything' has a designer. We don't know that for sure. NONE of us do. We KNOW that a watch and a car and a tractor have a designer, but it is a great leap in a logical argument to assume that, right off the bat, that EVERYTHING we see that looks designed must have been created. That flaw makes the #3 point above invalid, and the argument fails.

Another thing to consider is the enormous leap of point #2, in exclaiming that the universe looks like it has been designed. How (may I ask) do the designed features of a watch compare to the vastness of our universe? We know almost NOTHING about the universe, and EVERYTHING about a watch! David Hume (1711-1776) a famous Scottish philosopher reasoned similarly, in that he said, "for any comparison to make sense it should be made between 2 objects about which we have equal understanding."

A more complex thought around this argument is the fact that 'causation' can never be seen when (and if) it happens. The human mind, through past experience, will imagine a series of actions that possibly COULD have created a particular object. However, as we know very little of the whole (or the component parts) of the universe, how could we translate those thoughts to the possible creation of the universe?

In a sort of corollary, the sheer complexity of the universe does not really play a part in the assumption that it has been created, much to the dismay of theists who really LOVE this part. Take a car, for example. We know how cars are made. We can read books about it. We can even get someone to make a custom car FOR us. (From positiveatheism.org.) "If I showed you an egg and told you that I knew a man who made custom eggs, you would rightly doubt my word, for you've never seen an egg-maker. Thus the conclusion that a certain object was designed and made is based on the knowledge that such an object CAN be made, more than on the complexity of the object itself."

Theists love the so-called Anthropic Principle.

There are several versions of it and the originator of the principle by no means proposed it to be used to promote the theistic belief of a 'finely-tuned' universe by a creator, but it took, nonetheless. It is usually used in conjunction with an intelligent-designer argument, however there are some physicists and other scientists that, philosophically at least, see it as an interesting theory.

The basic idea is that the laws of nature in the universe have values that are consistent with conditions for life, as we know it, rather than a set of values that would not be consistent with life as observed on Earth. The thinking is that if the constants of the universe were, somehow, DIFFERENT than they are now, we would not be here to wonder about it all! The term rather misuses the term Anthropic, to mean humans, whereas all other forms of carbon-based life don't seem to be mentioned. This rather 'human-centric' view of the universe sits well with theists (as we are supposed to be the ultimate creation of god how do we know this, exactly?), but it is an easy point to take apart in a debate.

One important point to mention here (AGAIN, at the risk of repeating myself, but to good cause) is that one of the strongest-perceived arguments religious-minded people have FOR a creator of the universe is this 'finely-tuned' explanation of the physical constants, or the Laws of nature, which would include gravity, the strong nuclear force, etc. They state that scientists around the world agree, according to LEE STROBEL, a writer, creationist and Christian apologist, that "the universe and TIME ITSELF began with the BIG BANG." People, this is a theory that is constantly being worked on. NO-ONE KNOWS if that was the ultimate start, or one of many such starts in a vast 'multi-verse', or something that happens every trillion years. These are all theories that (due to the sheer complexity of observations and testable data and the sheer vastness of space) may NEVER be accepted as universal fact. The statement by Mr. Strobel argues that since the universe had a start (the BIG BANG) then "whatever begins to exist has a cause," and by logical inferences from the evidence "we can see that the universe is uncaused, timeless, immaterial, powerful, and personal. A pretty good starting point for the description of god." Ummm.... Which god was that again?

I said I would not go here, but I can't help myself (tee-hee).

Ray comfort (the star of a section of the previous chapter) famously used a banana to reveal its amazing 'perfection-of-design' features. With his ever-present side-kick KIRK CAMERON at his side, he begins by claiming the skin was easy to grab, the shape comfortable to hold, the fruit perfectly sized for our mouths, plus a 'pull-tab' to reveal the food beneath, all in an attempt to prove that where complex design is found, there must surely have been an intelligent designer who created it. I put this example in purely for comic relief, but it seems that Mr. Comfort was serious in his video (as he is a Christian minister, etc.) And it just goes to show you the length to which some people will go in the hopes of convincing the gullible amongst us that intelligent design is a valid theory of our existence. I wonder how his design-theory would explain the watermelon? I can barely pick a whole one up at the local supermarket!

In a sort of 'about face', the religious-minded sometimes refer to atheists as being fundamentalists.

This has been seen as a desperate measure by theists, claiming that atheism is a belief-system that allows ideas to be advanced by a position (faith?) that cannot be challenged or its statements tested. In professor Richard Dawkins case, he has been accused of being a shrill, strident fundamentalist, but rejects the charge whole-heartedly. He says he has a 'passion' for his work and his position on atheism and evolution, however this passion is often interpreted as a strident and shrill voice-of-knowing, much the same as could be attributed to, say, a zealous archbishop or priest. Dawkins sums it up nicely by the following comment: "The true scientist, however passionately he may 'believe', in evolution for example, knows exactly what would change his mind: evidence! The fundamentalist knows that nothing will."

It is perfectly okay to be angry and aggressive when face-to-face with a political opponent. One look at the goings-on in the Houses of Parliament in London will bear that out. Dedicated sports-fans can be especially mean to each other, as we have all witnessed on the television. These folks routinely get hot-under-the collar when discussing sports, and it's not all tongue-in-cheek as one might expect. Why, then, is religion essentially off limits to such criticism? It seems that religion has a firm foothold in a sacred, holy arena that can only be approached with kid gloves. "Peoples feelings will be hurt", is the usual argument. Why, I ask you, should people's feelings be hurt with words? Words are how we communicate. If I can't verbalize my position on critical-thinking and the hold religion has had on society these past 4,000 years how am I going to get my opinion out? For some reason religion is to be treated with a larger percentage of respect than other areas of our lives. I wonder if this is just another small way in which religion has found to prolong religious belief without criticism from non-believers? It seems patently true that faith (BLIND faith in this case) allows reason and rational thought to be applied to everything ELSE in ones life, except for ones own religious practices. When someone figures out why, please let me know.

I will now take some arguments from the theistic side recently heard on a riveting 2-hour debate pitching Christopher Hitchens against four theologians/authors, and see if there are any reasonable alternatives to their positions. It may be worth noting that they each had a three-minute closing statement and Hitchens was second-last. The final word came from Dr. William lane Craig, an American philosopher and theologian. This debate lasted 2 hours and his final 3 minutes were taken up by 10 arguments for Christian theism in which Craig states, "none of which have been responded to or refuted". Although Mr. Hitchens held up nicely in this overwhelmingly Christian arena, I believe this final statement was a bit non-essential, and seemed to whitewash over very explicit explanations and counter-arguments by Hitchens throughout the debate. Following are a couple of these arguments by Dr. Craig and why I think they are not valid ones.

Dr. Craig's first point is the argument of CONTINGENCY (part of the Cosmological argument). The main claim is that most of the things in the world around us are 'contingent', and these exist for a reason and should be able to be explained. .. WE are contingent, as if our parents never had us, we would not be here. We ARE here, so there has to be an explanation for being here. The universe may be contingent as well, so there must be an explanation for it. Theists call that thing 'GOD'. The reverse of this is things in our world which do exist that 'could not possibly have FAILED to exist'; things that ARE necessary; that do not have to be explained because their non-existence is impossible. One example is the Law of mathematics.

110

"Truths like 2 plus 2 being four would probably be true regardless of how the universe COULD have worked out, even if it had been radically different from the way we know it." Here is the summary of the ARGUMENT FROM CONTINGENCY:

(1) Everything that exists contingently has a reason for its existence

(2) The universe exists contingently, therefore:

(3) The universe has a reason for its existence.

(4) If the universe has a reason for its existence then that reason is god, therefore:

(5) God exists.

In my personal opinion this does not make a case for god. It is a great assumption that the universe is contingent, as theists claim. That there COULD have been a universe quite different from the one we know (even a nonexistent one!) is possible, but since we ARE here to observe what is going on, then I submit that, while we might be here contingently, we can't be THAT contingent, as supposedly god created man in his own image and that we are supposed to be one of his great accomplishments. If god had created a totally different universe, say, where WE DID NOT EXIST, there would be no humans to do his bidding, no humans to recognize his existence. The universe is the way it is because it is the way it is. We are humans, the way we are because of millions of years of natural selection. If the selection process went 'off' a few degrees along the way maybe humans would never have evolved, or we would be totally different from the way we are. Remember that we were almost wiped out several times as our numbers dwindled into the thousands a few times. Maybe we would have ended up with brains too small to even conjure up a supreme being (or even a religion, for that matter). To suggest that because we are 'contingent', therefore god must have created the universe, and us, to be here, is convoluted logic if I ever heard it.

The second point was the concept of morality. Dr. Craig says that without "a transcendent foundation there is no OBJECTIVE moral values, these are just the sociological, biological spin-offs of the evolutionary process". COME ON, Dr. Craig, give us all some credit. Technically, our moral actions could be attributed to a historical need to be cooperative amongst our tribe, but as well I rather say that in our world, solidarity amongst our species is PARAMOUNT to our happiness and productivity. Early societies would easily adapt to this. The 'objective' part of the argument only becomes important if you are trying to convince people of a god. That there can be no moral basis for our present-day morals WITHOUT a divine instigator is preposterous. Much evidence exists for other species being as cooperative. The fact that most of their behavior is INSTINCTUAL, I feel, is irrelevant. If a species (other than man) were to be involved in the most grotesque performance of 'sub-morality' against each other the species would have long ago been extinct. I suggest that could be one of the many reasons why, indeed, some of the more than 98% of all species that has ever existed, no longer exist.

That actually brings me to yet another interesting fact that theists seem to ignore, yet it falls squarely against their statements. I refer to the DESIGN THEORY that is constantly being raised at these debates, and on which I have touched on in previous chapters. So much is riding on this theory, and it amuses me how many facts, bold-faced as they be, are summarily ignored by even the most ardent theologian. Two points to consider when confronted by a 'design-theorist'; Point number one is the fact that over 95 percent of all the species of life this world has ever hosted has gone extinct. Some figure closer to over 98 percent. Anywhere from 75,000-200,000 years ago, we humans left the savannas of Africa for more northern climates. Enduring a possible 'nuclear winter', resulting from the TOBA super-volcano around 70,000 years ago, and other possible threats, the human population has been estimated to have gone down to less than 15,000 worldwide. This, perhaps, was only the most recent catastrophic event that made humans a potentially endangered species. Some experts proffer a theory that the numbers of humans and our ancestors were chronically low throughout the last two million years, sometimes with only 10,000 breeding individuals surviving. I make these points to illustrate the ridiculous notion that we have an all-seeing, all-knowing, perfect god that designed this earth just for us, yet we almost became extinct a number of times throughout our relatively brief history. Great design, huh??

It is also worth noting that the possibility of life on other planets probably does exist (it may sound like I am digressing, but bear with me) due to the immense amount of galaxies that make up our known universe. The rest of them, trillions, in fact, are simply inhospitable and uninhabitable. None of the planets in our own solar system are habitable and most of our OWN planet is this way too. About 70 percent of our orb is covered by water averaging several thousand feet in depth. Around 20 percent of the earth is cold/hot desert (Antarctica included) and that leaves a very small percentage of land available for all of us to squabble over. AGAIN, some design. One would have thought that if there WERE a god who created our planet for us that he would have conceived a complete paradise, rather than the scrappy, barely habitable piece of rock that it is.

Here is another argument from theism that relates to the 'fine-tuning' of the universe. Of course, they call it fine-tuning because they want atheists from the very beginning to acknowledge that it is an entity that is doing the 'tweaking' of all the natural laws we know about. The laws like Newton's law of universal gravitation, conservation of energy, laws from fluid mechanics, planetary motion, etc. Are available for all to read on. The theists claim that if just one of the many laws of nature were to have been tweaked just minutely, we would not have existed at all. The one thing theists seem to forget is that we ARE here, and that means that whatever state the natural laws have in place, THAT is the state we need in order for us to have a functioning solar-system and universe, and for us to be here to talk about it.

I now take the greatest of pleasure in offering you a tidbit from a website that states in their 'about us' section http://The4thDayAlliance.com is a "non-profit religious organization dedicated to proclaiming the Glory of God through astronomy."' That's a new one for me. After reading an article from David Rives Ministries contained on their site, regarding 'earth's habitable zone' I was immediately drawn to the fact that the information they provide is proof obvious for the materialist side of things, rather than the theistic. The article brings TWO types of habitable 'zones' to consider, the GALACTIC, and the CIRCUM-STELLAR. The Galactic Habitable zone refers to our distance from the center of our own spiraling galaxy (a black hole where everything near the event horizon gets sucked in, never to be seen again) allowing us to reside safely, out of harms way. This, they say, is a great argument FOR the existence of god; that he placed us at just the perfect location in our galaxy so as not to succumb to the finality of the big, bad, black hole.

Let me interrupt myself here for a second, and point out that these folks seem to be getting things backwards. They use Astronomy to proclaim the glory of god, yet they claim they know everything about the universe and it's creation. Maybe not the details, but *they are proclaiming god's existence and then uttering a collective 'wow' when they view the heavens through a telescope*. Again, how does what we are looking at (and I assume we all see the same stuff up there) PROVE the existence of god exactly? The big difference here (and one of the most important in the theist/atheist debates) is the fact that theists KNOW God created everything and use empirical science discoveries to 'prove' their claim. Atheists, on the other hand, claim to know NOTHING, and intelligently go about the scientific process to see 'what's up'. Let's continue:

"The Circum-stellar (or the solar system's) habitable zone is a description of our planet being just the correct distance from our sun so that we may have life".. Five percent closer and we all fry; twenty percent further away and we all start learning how to ice-fish. I suppose the simple fact that the Andromeda galaxy is speeding towards us at break-neck speed ON A COLLISION COURSE, guaranteeing annihilation of earth in 5 billion years, escapes them? At the risk of sounding repetitive, SOME DESIGN, HUH?

The real icing-on-the-cake comes at the end of this brief article when a quote from the bible is given. This may be the only quote of the bible you will see in my book (apart from the chapter where I take the old and new testament to task), but this one is worth its weight in space-dust. Considering the tenuous position of our earth with respect to the sun; the relative un-inhabitability of it; the fact that man has almost gone extinct numerous times throughout our history and suffers natural disasters on a weekly basis today, I hardly think it beneficial to the theistic side to include this profound quote in their article. Here is that quote, from Isaiah 45:18 "For thus saith the LORD that created the heavens; God himself that formed the earth and made it; he hath established it, he created it not in vain, he formed it to be inhabited: I am the LORD; and there is none else." Ever heard of the phrase try harder?

Finally (but surely not the only other one out there) here is another of the more common theistic arguments for the subsistence (ontology) of God.

1) ONTOLOGICAL

The actual study of this could give one perpetual headaches trying to figure out some of the 'reductio ad absurdum' arguments and the use of SYMBOLIC LOGIC to promote the idea that god really exists.. I will give a very light version here, so the basics can be understood.

It is said that it is possible to imagine a perfect being that exists, and the Judeo-Christian call that being, GOD. IF this being is so perfect, then, by very definition, that being must necessarily exist in all possible worlds. The second premise of this argument is that it is at least possible, then, for god to exist. The conclusion is that god exists.

You can delve far more deeply into this argument, as it has its grounding in various forms of LOGIC and other areas. At the end of the day I am inclined to give a very short answer to the whole argument, and that is to say that 'You cannot define or imagine a thing into existence.' I STILL find that even the logical arguments don't address the simple fact that our basic knowledge of god comes from man-written holy books. Why can't these learned folks use basic logic on THAT statement? Here, then, is MY 'logical' argument, for what it's worth:

1) Man wrote the bible and made up all the stories, so

2) Everything IN the bible is the word of man.

3) It is said in the bible that everything in the bible is from 'the word of god'.then,

4) God exists only in the bible and as the word of man.

Therefore,

5) GOD DOES NOT EXIST IN REALITY!!

A basic argument, maybe not so technically correct but just as reasonable as others out there.

CHAPTER Eleven

A little faith is all you need

Ahhh, faith. Blind faith. The one thing theists would have to admit is the only force keeping religion alive (if atheists had their way!). It is safe to say that, here in the United States, the majority of us have a belief in a religion (Christianity dominates), with about 20-30 million atheists. However, in a new book by Stephen Prothero, Religious Literacy, he gives us two rather unsettling statistics. The first is that we are the most religious nation in the developed world. The second (and most disturbing) is that we are the most religiously ignorant people in the western world. Less than half of us can identify Genesis as the first book of the Bible, and only one third know that Jesus delivered the Sermon on the Mount. And you call yourselves Christian!

Why do I think this is important? Look, people. It is one thing to stand up for a religion you believe in. That is what these debates are about.

We need intelligent discourse amongst people that have a passion for their respective views on religion. How is it, then, that over 50% of the bible-thumping public cannot know of some of the basic teachings and stories of the bible? What exactly are you believing in, people? Are you really that scared of life and insecure about your existence and ability to affect change in your own circumstances that you simply go along with everyone else? For the first time since researching this book I am really feeling sorry for a whole lot of folks right now. I don't intend to be mean, but this is truly sad to me. I am not a pillar of strength. I have my emotional weaknesses and baggage to deal with. I prefer to be by myself than with someone. Less complicated and more freedom that way, I feel. I digress but I can't imagine the extent of personal weakness that someone must endure to allow them to be horn-swoggled by the whole religious thing.

At this point I would like to substitute the word 'superstition' for the word 'faith'. It is the most reasonable attempt I can muster to place a meaningful description of the practice of living by one's religion in today's world. I don't see it any other way. It is true, I will admit, that religion is somewhat 'hard-wired' into us humans. That is self-evident by the past 4,000 years of human history. I use the word 'superstition' because I do not want to sound ambiguous. So you can see how this word fits religious belief to a tee, here are the first two definitions of the word from the online Merriam-Webster dictionary. These were the first two definitions I found I did not cherry-pick.

1 a: "a belief or practice resulting from ignorance, fear of the unknown, trust in magic or chance, or a false conception of causation

b : an irrational abject attitude of mind toward the supernatural, nature, or God resulting from superstition". And

2: "A notion maintained despite evidence to the contrary".

With all due respect to my fellow men and women, these two definitions support my position on why people come to believe in religion. It is wrong, and potentially destructive, especially to those who take religion a bit more seriously than others (NOT a small percentage, I remind you). Is there anything in these two that you don't understand? Taken with the second statistic in the first paragraph above, definition number one seems like an amazing fit, does it not?

I can see that a few of you who are reading this book might be wondering why I bother to write this at all? It's not that I can change history by trying to 'convert' a few people to a more reasoned-based existence. It's not as though I have some major alternative to those unfortunate enough to somehow need, desperately, their religious connections. I just think that the natural world is too amazing and wonderful to have your heads stuck in a cloud somewhere, hoping Jesus will make your life better and wash away your sins 'in the tide'. I have to say that I simply hope that I can knock some sense into a few of you that have 'TRULY lost your way.'

Endeavor to debate a theist on the subject of faith and you will surely have him/her start by making a statement to the effect that we need faith in everyday life. Our futures are uncertain, so we need a degree of blind faith to give us hope. You have faith that the lobster you just ordered will be cooked properly so as to avoid certain gastrointestinal discomforts. You have faith in your schoolteachers that they are giving you a decent education. All true, but let's not kid ourselves. As with the Ontological argument for god's existence (and many other old, tired, refuted ones) words can have different meanings.

I can hardly think that any intellectual theist is going to equate having faith in a bus getting to one's stop on time with faith in a supernatural sky-god. Are you talking to a 5 year-old here? That one CAN'T fool people.

C.S. Lewis said that "most of the things you believe are believed on authority, secondary evidence, etc. For example, you may never have actually seen a living dinosaur, but you are confident based on evidence that dinosaurs once existed." This may be as far as the religious majority might go, with the corollary thinking that since 100's of millions of other people believe there is a god. There must be. Mr. Lewis concludes by saying "Of course, experience and rational investigation should increase your confidence in what is true." Well, sir, with all due respect, that does not seem to be happening in the religious community.

I am now on a website (http://www.faithfacts.org.) that states "*This website is all about using reason and evidence to examine ultimate things. First we will examine how faith fits into the use of reason and evidence in such exploration.*" A noble and at the same time a rather futile exploit. However, a bit further down on the first page discussing faith, it blows all critical-thinking out of the proverbial window.

"*The real issue is what is a worthy object of our faith. In this section of our website we will show that Christianity is reasonable and rational, that it is logically consistent, that it fits the evidence, and that it is relevant for modern man.*" Looks like we atheists have our work cutout for us. I feel that it is important to stay with this website for a while, as it tries to convince us of things that do not stand up. Here are some statements by this site and my criticisms of them.

1) *"Note to the skeptic who is willing to delve into religion based on reason and evidence: Human beings have imperfect knowledge. There are always things outside the realm of our experience. So we often base our perception of things on assumptions or "presuppositions," either consciously or unconsciously. But we must be careful not to become prisoners of our preconceptions. There is always the possibility that some new information could overturn our previous ideas."* This last underlined statement is a parallel thought that most intelligent atheists take to heart. As stated earlier, no true atheist can claim 100% knowledge of there being no god. To be a true critical-thinker one MUST allow a couple of percentage points in favor of some FUTURE evidence that might prove the existence of a supernatural being. Truthfully, we do so really to be respectful of the majority theist camp. We don't really think there will be any such evidence. Really.

Obviously we don't know everything. Science, the best vehicle we humans have to increase our knowledge in many areas of life, is continually expanding our understanding of the world around us. We are fallible, and some of us DO have pre-conceptions of things. The true rational person, however, using critical-thinking and evidence as presented by the brightest minds of our human race, does not need faith (in the religious sense) to believe something is true. The underlined last sentence above is way truer of science than it is of religion. Religious beliefs HAVE progressed as well through time, mainly by way of mass education and the huge contributions to society by the secular community (slave abolishment, emancipation of women, etc.), but we still have religion in a big way. I don't know why. If there are things that concern us "outside the realm of our experience", then we should assume that the thing in question will be neither true nor false and let evidence and reason be the determinant, not mass superstition and the entrenchment of a religious doctrine over time.

2) "*We argue that you may have claimed the right to judge the rationality and morality of things. But consider that apart from God you cannot make any of your claims stick beyond your own subjective state. This is so because you cannot explain rationality itself. Why do the laws of logic seem to work? Who says so? Why do we all have moral ideas about right and wrong and the desire to impose them? Why do we expect nature to act uniformly?*"

Let's take the last sentence first. We expect nature to act uniformly because if it did not, we would not likely be here to discuss it. The 'uniformity' of things comes about when one has a naturally occurring universe that has, for eventual good or bad (for us humans) lasted for billions of years. Even the non-educated among us knows what to expect when they wake up in the morning. So far, this solar system of ours has done us proud over the last number of eons and let's hope it continues, at least until the proximity of the Andromeda galaxy gets too close and we all fry.

We (atheists, I assume) do not claim the sole right to judge rationality and morals. We simply assert that it is man's natural ability to have and NEED solidarity amongst ourselves and, as such, we have evolved an innate, 'you-scratch-my-back-and-I'll-scratch-yours' mentality. It's only religious indoctrination and despotic, land-hungry commanders and their armies that have destroyed man's moral reputation here on earth over the centuries. I submit that our 'subjective' state is all that is needed. I can behave nicely WITHOUT god. I DO, and always HAVE done. Many others do too. YOU cannot explain rationality as well, yet you presume to tell me I have this 'father-in-the-heavens' that determines what I do and how I'm supposed to do it. An irrational belief in order to garner for yourself an 'objective' set of moral laws is disturbing, to say the least. I think I'll give that one a miss, if you don't mind.

3) "*When the unbeliever uses logic against Christianity, he implicitly acknowledges a God who   grants us logic*!"

I can't believe the writer had the audacity to use an exclamation mark at the end of that sentence! Logic itself is a complex undertaking, and tries to use deductive and inductive reasoning to find out what is true and what is false. There is also synthesis and analysis of problems and the study of logic can be quite an intellectual undertaking. It is a misstatement to say that atheists use logic to disprove the existence of god. Why bother? We don't use or need logic to prove the nonexistence of many things. Ghosts, elephants with wings, Bertrand Russell's teapot. You-name-it. In fact it is the theists that routinely place the ontological and teleological arguments and more in front of the atheists, ultimately to no avail. The biggest mistake in #3 above (tired I am of seeing this time and time again) is the assumption that god exists. THAT IS THE THING WE ARE ALL TRYING TO PROVE/DISPROVE SO THERE CAN BE NO ASSUMPTIONS PLEASE! Try to stop your faith from getting in the way of reasoned thinking,

Is that so much to ask?

CHAPTER Twelve

"SHOW ME THE EVIDENCE"

This chapter will focus more on Darwin's Theory of evolution by natural selection, rather that the origins of our universe. This topic of debate is undeniably the most contested when pitting theists with evolutionists. Essentially, the theists have a 'bone' to pick with evolutionists and biologists, whenever they mention the word 'Evolution'. Some even laugh when respected scientists suggest that they take a simple trip to their local museum to see at least some fossil evidence of a certain species' progression.

There should actually be no rift between the two. There should be no reason why theists should ignore and deny the evolutionary fact. Indeed, there is a fair number who agree with it, they just don't agree with the 'naturally-occurring' idea. It is quite conceivable to me that even the most devout theologian could embrace the fact of evolution and use it as a positive addition to the glory of the god he worships (whichever one that is). Why should these two parties not come together and shake hands? Well, maybe it's because science and religion look at the world in different ways. Science is 'all about the evidence' and uses concrete, testable elements; forms hypotheses and has the whole scientific community standing on the precipice, just waiting to prove them wrong. That is if they CAN! The more theories are judged, challenged and scrutinized and found to be justified, the more the theory is considered correct. The longer it stays around without being corrected or proven wrong to any degree, the scientific community accepts it as fact. Facts CAN change over time to be sure. With new technologies and equipment, vast improvement in our knowledge increases each year. In this case, evolution IS A SCIENTIFIC concept, and can make no assumptions or opinions relating to a super-natural creator. Conversely, religion is all about faith and the study of ancient, man-made, 'hard-to-get-the-extracted-meaning-out-of' books created 2,000 years ago by an ancient civilization and has nothing to do with evidence. Was that a jab? Sorry. Only kidding. What I MEANT to say is that religion *'invokes super-natural explanations that cannot be tested*,' and that through that, it sees the world in a different light. As I see it, the two areas do not have to be incompatible, as the religious-minded can agree on evolution without compromising their core beliefs.

This powerful theory explains much of the way we are, and how we began. Fossils show the preserved history of life. It shows us how we are similar, and different, from other species. It also shows us where certain species were distributed past and present. As I have stated before, many scientific disciplines come together in giving us a vast amount of evidence for this theory. Today, new and exciting DNA and GENOME projects are hard at work showing that we are all connected in some way. I believe these last two items somehow get swept under the rug when antagonists of the theory ask 'show me the evidence'. Quite learned folks seem to leave out mentioning these new and exciting technologies when asking that question. We will leave that for a bit later.

Mainly they are asking, perhaps quite rightly, where is all this 'mountain' of evidence you have for your evolutionary theory? OK then. I will attempt to put in concise terms what the evolutionary theory states and a bit of information on the actual physical observation of fossil remains, and how scientists are able to link these together. Perhaps the best introduction to this subject would be a look at the first paragraph of the Paleontological

125

Societies position statement on Evolution. The paragraph begins:

"Evolution is both a scientific fact and a scientific theory. Evolution is a fact in the sense that life has changed through time. In nature today, the characteristics of species are changing, and new species are arising. The fossil record is the primary factual evidence for evolution in times past, and evolution is well documented by further evidence from other scientific disciplines, including comparative anatomy, biogeography, genetics, molecular biology, and studies of viral and bacterial diseases. Evolution is also a theory, an explanation for the observed changes in life through Earth history that has been tested numerous times and repeatedly confirmed. Evolution is an elegant theory that explains the history of life through geologic time; the diversity of living organisms, including their genetic, molecular, and physical similarities and differences; and the geographic distribution of organisms. Evolutionary principles are the foundation of all basic and applied biology and paleontology, from biodiversity studies to studies on the control of emerging diseases." There you go.

A little bit of an explanation of exactly what a 'species' is, might be applicable here, as most people are interested in the creation, or progression, of new species throughout the evolutionary time-frame. I do reference this in another part of the book, but here it is again, for clarification. Basically, a species is a group of organisms that can interbreed and create viable offspring. *"In other words, a species can have babies that can have babies, and so on. It has been falsely put forward that a MULE is a new species. No, it is not. When a donkey and a horse mate, one gets a mule. The buck stops there, unfortunately, as mules are sterile and cannot continue the bloodline. HUMANS, although cosmetically and superficially can be quite varied, are extremely close genetically and can, of course, interbreed making us a*

126

uniform species. Why our external characteristics ARE so varied (skin color, nose-shape, hair formations and color, etc.) and yet our internal genetics so similar? I don't know if even scientists have an answer for that yet."

Here, in this chapter, and In a previous one, I explained that a theory gets developed and challenged at all stages until it is accepted as fact, and that is the case with evolution. It is not a bunch of scientists getting together in a 'boys club' and having only a few fossil remains and claiming linkage between them. As a theory, evolution *"must continue to be open to testing"*. So far, it has undergone 150 years of such scrutiny and present-day technologies are addressing even *"more fruitful inquiries"* based on *"the tempo and mode of evolution, the various processes involved in evolution, and the driving factors for evolution. Through such inquiry, the unifying theory of evolution will become an even more powerful explanation for the history of life on Earth."*

Before I go on it is worth noting that there is research that is being done in many areas of the fossil record. Apparently there is interest in the concept of how certain species managed to survive past 'mass extinctions' and what type of traits would one have to have over the other to make it through. Was it just luck? Was it a larger geographical 'spread-out' of the related species group that made some of them survive? It is an interesting thought, and one that has added a new dimension to evolutionary theory.

The most common thinking in the 'Natural Selection' process is that it is one that tends to improve the survival characteristics of a certain species, *"weeding out organisms with traits not quite suited to a particular environment, favoring those with traits slightly better for promoting survival and reproduction"*. It is argued, by Dr. David Jablonski, a Paleontologist at the University of Chicago, that most of the traits we see in species today probably are not there for ultimate survival through the very tough times. Most of these "*beautiful adaptations will be lost, not because they are poorly adapted to the vast bulk of evolutionary time, but because they happen not to be linked to the kind of factors that promote survival during those short-lived but intense mass extinctions.*" This, perhaps, can be viewed as obvious but it does promote an interesting area of study that adds to the general understanding and development of present-day evolutionary theory.

Let me digress for a second and say that some theists find the process of evolution too 'random' and 'violent' to be something one would attribute to something God would conjure up. Far from being random (with the exception of genes and their mutations on individual organisms) it truly is a 'survival-of-the-fittest' scenario, and very violent, indeed, with each successive generation of species trying to survive the best way they can. One can hardly blame other species for being violent, protecting themselves from harm and possible extinction. Look at the great lengths we humans have gone to fight our enemies and to hack away at the environment, all in an effort to prolong our species. Violent, indeed. The fact that some theists refuse to accept evolution BECAUSE of its inherent violent nature is ignoring the very basis of HUMAN nature. We need to survive, no matter what, and are ready to do whatever is necessary to achieve it. Maybe that does not seem like the idea a loving creator would have had when setting out to produce us, but those are the breaks.

To let you all know what theists 'generally' accept and what is perhaps not is explained in this way. You may hear mention of two areas in Evolutionary debates, namely "micro-evolution" and "macro-evolution". The accepted former concept talks about a small-scale change in the genetic 'make-up' BENEATH the main 'species' level. For interest, this comes about by several processes like, mutation, natural selection, and genetic drift. The disputed main part of evolutionary theory (by THEISTS not scientists) is the 'macro' concept of the origin of 'higher organisms'. *Another term for macro-evolution could be called "descent with modification" There is much in dispute about what actually constitutes a 'higher organism', but we shall say that it is one of the main species we all recognize today, they having characters in common that make them different from other organisms.*" Clear? This macro-evolution includes common ancestry, the relation of all life to one another, and more. Theists have an even larger 'bone' to throw because evolutionists call this well-scientifically-supported view as a 'fact of evolution'. A fact it is, however to theists, that may sound too final.

Finding fossils is not easy. "*Cambrian rock strata, the oldest and most dinosaur and invertebrate-filled type of rock around, has revealed only a relatively small number of animal fossilizations, compared to all types of species that must have lived up to 600 million years ago.*" The current problem with these fossils is that, (according to creationists), there are not enough intermediary fossils showing a gradual change in evolution, as many biologists state as the way evolution works. One of the only alternative theories that evolutionists can come up with is that natural selection changes happened in large 'spurts', rather that incrementally. There are exceptions to this, as several examples exist that could explain an intermediary in these very old fossils. It is fair to point out that the last 20 years has yielded much more fossil evidence from which scientists can study. I may be repeating myself, but this is a good spot to add that whenever the scientific community comes up with a fossil intermediate between two species, the theists shout that there is now TWO MORE gaps in the fossil record, whereas before there was only one. Sounds like a never-ending story. It would be impossible to find every fossil for every possible change in the evolutionary progression in a species. The best we can hope for are finds that represent a rather significant change in a species over time, in order to get a better understanding of the ultimate 'direction' of a particular lineage.

"During Darwin's lifetime, a fossilized species was discovered which appeared to be intermediate between a bird and a reptile. It had feathers like a bird, but a toothed jaw like a reptile. He named it an Archaeopteryx. It seemed to be just the kind of intermediate form which Darwin's theory predicted, and was taken as good evidence for evolution. This helps a lot because recently, fossils of feathered dinosaurs have been discovered that might suggest a link between Archaeopteryx and the Theropod dinosaur. The Theropod group is very diverse and runs from the large T-REX to smaller, flying dinosaurs. One reason why it is difficult to obtain these remains is that they are, indeed rare, and in the case of smaller specimens, their smaller bones wither away, leaving very little (if any) trace."

To the uninitiated it might appear that evolutionists seem to be waffling between this theory and that explanation. It is only that the business of evolution is so challenging and includes contributions from Paleobiology, geology and organic chemistry (how living organisms have evolved) as well as ecology, genetics and molecular biology that attempt to "demonstrate how living species are currently changing in response to their environments and therefore undergoing evolution." Many more sub-disciplines are involved, as well as new concepts relating to the ever-improving technology fields.. Anyone rationally delving into exactly what it takes to prove linkages between fossils in the record will come away awestruck indeed by the massive undertaking it is.

Ray J. Egan

An explanation of NATURAL SELECTION should be placed here for your enjoyment. It is the basic foundation for the study of the most elegant 'family-tree' of all the species, and the main driving force behind Darwin's Theory of evolution. Some dispute over the actual percentage that natural selection HAS over evolution exists (compared to other factors), but it is the driving force behind it. Other mechanisms of evolution can also include mutation, migration and 'genetic drift' but we will leave the discussion to the basics. There are three main areas where an individual organism might survive and continue to evolve, thereby having 'natural selection' as the outcome. These three are VARIATION, DIFFERENTIAL REPRODUCTION, and HEREDITY. Here is a basic example and a description of the three areas as we go:

1) "*Within certain species you will find there are certain VARIATIONS in some traits. Some variations can occur within a certain species by POLYMORPHISM, in which individuals can exhibit different structures, colors and biochemistry but CLEARLY belong to the same species, as they reproduce with one another*" (again, a major element of determining whether two organisms are from the same species).

Another way in which variation can occur is by GEOGRAPHIC variation. Sometimes there is no obvious pattern to these changes, but in CLINAL variation it is interesting to note that this can be a gradual change in some feature, depending on geography. From the Freeman and Herron book (2001) chapter 12, the interesting part is that "*in the northern hemisphere you frequently find that populations of mammals are smaller in the south and gradually as you go north you find that within a species the individuals are larger and larger. Such a pattern of gradual change is called a cline so this form of variation is called clinal variation.*"

131

The final variation is with those species within certain HYBRID zones. An example of this would be red-shafted and yellow-shafted flickers (birds). On the east coast of the U.S. you get mainly yellow and the west coast the red-shafted flicker. There is a "convergence-zone" of a few hundred miles where there is a proliferation of both types. SPECIATION is a very complicated area, so these examples will have to suffice.

2) DIFFERENTIAL REPRODUCTION can be likened to the concept of 'survival of the fittest', and is really the ESSENCE of the natural selection process. A very good example of this comes from http://www.library.thinkquest.com and it goes like this: "Differential reproduction is the idea that those organisms best adapted to a given environment will be most likely to survive to reproductive age and have offspring of their own. Organisms that are successful in their environments will be more likely to be successful in reproduction, and therefore the better-adapted organisms will reproduce at a greater rate than the less well-adapted organisms." In one example, consider a snow-covered habitat where there are both white and brown-furred small animals that are constantly preyed upon. In this case (the quote goes on to state) "the white-furred animals are less likely to be seen by predators and are therefore more likely to survive. Thus, more white-furred animals will make it to reproductive age and have offspring, who will most likely share their genes for white fur. Therefore white fur will come to dominate the population. Differential reproduction, or difference in the rates of reproduction of differently-adapted organisms, will favor the better-adapted organisms at the expense of the worse-adapted ones." This IS getting interesting, don't you think?

3) The third area that natural selection can be observed is the idea of HEREDITY. This is defined as the transmission of character traits from the

parents to their offspring. VARIATION also occurs when discussing heredity, as I will state here. From HUBPAGES.com we get this explanation of how heredity works:

"Characters of parents get copied in children. Skin color, hair color, height, appearance, etc. In children resemble either of parents or grandparents. This phenomenon is known as heredity."

"Chromosomes contain genes, which work like a recording device, recording all the genetic codes of an individual and transferring them to the next generation."

"Variation: As half of the chromosomes come from the paternal side and the other half from maternal side, so the offspring will have a mix of characters from both parents. This mixing up of characters creates slight variation in the genetic makeup of the offspring. These variations accumulate over hundreds of years giving rise to an altogether new species."

Lets take a hypothetical beetle as an example, and use the above information as a guide. From http://www.evolution.berkeley.edu we can assume that, within the particular species of beetle, that some are brown and some are green. These would be the VARIATION IN CHARACTER TRAITS. "*There is also differential reproduction. Since the environment can't support unlimited population growth, not all individuals get to reproduce to their full potential. In this example, green beetles tend to get eaten by birds and survive to reproduce less often than brown beetles do. There is heredity. The surviving brown beetles have brown baby beetles because this trait has a genetic basis. End result: The more advantageous trait, brown coloration, which allows the beetle to have more offspring, becomes more common in the population. If this process continues, eventually, all individuals in the population will be brown.*" 'Elegant, indeed

It is well worth noting that some fairly recent discoveries have shown that sometimes evolution can actually be seen, and I will site some examples of this in a later chapter.

Natural selection is a fact. Just as it is a fact that the earth rotates around the sun (the last statement proving that science works as time progresses by people challenging these ideas - even if theists put those newly-challenged idea-people in jail for it (Galileo).

There are 15 very captivating examples of changes within certain species I would like to show to you. Unfortunately, for this author, it is rather expensive to include them in this book, so I will invite all of you to search for '15 evolutionary Gems' on the internet. They will amaze you all.

I thought these 15 examples really underscored the importance of science delving even further into evolutionary theory. If one does a little research one will find that there is a MOUNTAIN of evidence out there to support the idea of macro and micro-evolution. In reality it would take a lifetime to study all that is involved in our complex 'family tree'. I, for one, am glad that we have the best and brightest minds looking into this. One day we will have so much obvious evidence that theists will unanimously come together to support the idea of evolution.

Reason, and evidence, might win out after all..

CHAPTER Thirteen

Intelligent 'Design' in the classroom?

It might best be stated right-off-the-bat, according to the United States Supreme Court, that the teaching of Creationism as science in public schools is unconstitutional. A lower court, in Dover, Texas, also ruled that intelligent design should not be presented as an alternative explanation to Darwin's ⊨ Theory of evolution.

It is quite clear that the first amendment to the Constitution has a general principle of 'church and state separation'. From http://www.religioustolerance.org as interpreted by the Courts, the Constitution's First Amendment requires that public school teachers, principals, and boards be religiously neutral:

- They may not promote a particular religion as being superior to any other.

- They may not promote religion in general as superior to a secular approach to life.

- They may not be antagonistic to religion in general or a particular religious belief in particular.

- They may not be antagonistic to secularism.

- They must neither advance nor inhibit religion.

This conflict between the Church and state has been brewing for centuries. The really interesting thing about our own constitution is that the Framers (the delegates to the Federal Convention who took part in 'framing' or drafting the proposed Constitution of the United States) were mainly from the Protestant side of Christianity. The funny thing is that there were around 6 different sects represented by these folks, and they were about as different (the style and methods of their worship) as the Hindus are to the Muslims or Jews. None of them wanted the other sects to eventually gain control of the government so every effort was made to make religion as benign as possible in drafting the Constitution.

The current law also prohibits public schools from putting one denomination or religion ahead of, or at the expense of, another faith group or secular philosophy. For example, a comparative religion class must give a balanced description of religious and secular beliefs from a variety of faith groups and ethical systems. This law also prevents students from being required to recite prayers in class. One of the potential problems that would exist if a school WERE to allow such prayers would be the harassment and abuse by fellow students. Some state laws allowing this type of prayer sometimes permit the non-religious student to wait outside the classroom until the prayers are over. Children have ENOUGH to deal with in school without being potentially ostracized in this way.

Also (from http://www.religioustolerance.org) one runs the risk of religious indoctrination. "*The 1st amendment of the U.S. constitution states that there shall be no law regarding the establishment of religion. The courts view prayer in the classroom to be one example of the government approving one religion over another. Even a student-selected, student-given, non-sectarian, non-proselytizing prayer still carries with it the stamp of approval of the state - i.e. the state approves of, and is seen to promote, belief in God (and whatever other religious content that the prayer might have).*"

Having said that, there are several ways in which religion has been passed down from generation to subsequent generation throughout the ages. Family ties offer the best way of indoctrinating children from a very early age. Please, don't take offense at my use of that word, however, as I am an atheist and simply demand of society that the adults keep their beliefs to themselves until the child is of an age where they can be exposed to many different religions. It is simply unfair to them. It is also arrogant to think that YOUR particular god (regardless of whether everyone ELSE in your community is of the same belief) is the only one, the best one, or not. A person should be able to intelligently choose what is best for him/her at the age he or she can make those decisions on the cosmos, humanity, and religion. To believe one needs the religion of the parents to somehow succeed in the community just because 'everyone else is doing it' is weak justification. I would have thought a child that has been brought up to be a critical thinker and one who uses reason would fare far better in this world.

I suppose it is logical, however, to assume that if you grow up in Northern Ireland, for example, that you turn out to be either Catholic or Protestant. If you really think about it, using modern world reason you MIGHT be able to see why that would be the case in ancient times. One would think though, that as a loving parent, you would not want you offspring to be hindered by a belief in any one religion. The fact that the parent's belief is strong is one thing. That's a decision THEY made. The fact that their parents brought them up that way does not mean they have to continue the trend. Can't people think for themselves? This really does bother me for some reason. Labeling a child a 'Catholic' child or a 'Hindu' child in these modern times is inexcusable. Religion can simply be taken too far. It's one thing to believe in the overall stories and revere something that is believed to be on a higher plane than yourself, but leave it at that.... for yourself. One of the main assumptions our society makes, regardless of whether we are religious or not, that we all buy into the convention that children belong to the religion of the parents. Professor Richard Dawkins goes on to say that this labeling of children could be considered a "*mild form of child abuse*". By the way, if you would like an interesting look at one example of how this MAY be considered child abuse, you may have fun looking at this video on YouTube. Type in the search-bar the following 'why religion is child abuse'. "Whew" is the only thing I said after I saw that one.

Unfortunately, this early education can be found in many school districts around the world. Classes that teach religion are fairly common, although mainly in areas where religion really does have a prominent foothold. I don't remember having an option to take religious studies in either junior or senior high school in Canada. Maybe we are ahead of the curve up there. Public schools serve children from a variety of religious and philosophical backgrounds. The classroom is an inappropriate place for school-sponsored worship therefore, in my opinion.

I feel the same way when people ask me what I think about prayers at graduation ceremonies or whether public school sports teams should be allowed to pray together. I think it should be an enormous assumption that the members of a team should all be of the same denomination (with the exception of, I guess, regions of fundamentalism) and equally brutal to think that they should all sit through a prayer that has nothing to do with their own families beliefs, especially now with the diversity experienced here in the United States. If ANYTHING should be assumed, it is that you might have 5 different religions represented on the same team, and that the proper thing would not to have a prayer at all but perhaps a rousing, secular chant or something. In fact, various courts have made past rulings that would tend to agree with my position. This also goes hand-in-hand with what I was saying earlier, that a one-sided religious approach, where children are concerned, is wrong. Just like parents should teach their children about ALL religions (or none) so should the schools.

Another point from www.religiioustolerance.org states that: "*teachers, coaches, etc. cannot lead a group prayer. To do so would be viewed as school endorsement of a specific religion, which is unconstitutional under the principle of separation of church and state.*" The second point is "*student led, student written public prayers are not permitted to be part of a game format, i.e. the school officials cannot insert a prayer into the schedule of a game, even if the actual prayer is led by a student.*"

From the RELIGION TODAY news summary, 1999-MAR-19 even the Board of Education is limited in it's scope of religious practice. "*The 6th U.S. Circuit Court of appeals decided on 1999-MAR-18 that the Board of Education in Cleveland, OH, couldn't pray before their meetings. The court ruled that prayers are an illegal endorsement of religion. School board attorneys have not decided whether they will appeal the case to the U.S. Supreme Court.*"

Interesting to mention here that there is also a percentage of young people, brought up in primarily fundamentalist areas in the United States, who are literally under pressure from their peers and pastors AND family members to stay put. What I mean by this is that a cultish mentality sometimes exists in communities where people simply want to get out from under the clutches of their communities' religion and go on to other things. I am not saying that all fundamentalist communities are cults, but I WOULD state that a literal belief in the scriptures, pure blind faith plus the apparent rejection of reason would certainly make one stop and think. This atmosphere of 'benign coercion' makes it very difficult for the child to know where, and who, to turn to for advice and help. The same opinion, from http://www.allabouthistory.org, is the concept that *"school prayer is inherently coercive and cannot be implemented in a way that is truly voluntary. What young child could regard prayer as voluntary where it is lead by his teacher, incorporated into the school routine and engaged in by the majority of his peers?"*

One other reason I feel why religion should be left out of the classroom is that public schools are public and that private prayer or religious practice should be left out of it. The public school system is for ALL children, and on any given day (here in the United States) one might see the children of Catholic, agnostic, Islamist, Baptist, Jewish and atheist parents in these schools. Taxpayers support these schools as well, so they should be free from anything religious.

Again (for the record) school prayer is unconstitutional. You will find, in the establishment clause of the First Amendment that *"government shall make no law respecting the establishment of religion."* As stated above, because most schools are public-funded, prayers led by school officials would have to be considered 'government-established religion'. Consequently a 'no-no'.

In reading many of the arguments FOR prayers in public schools, I found them not to be so convincing. The majority of them say that religion in schools would teach and influence moral values, combat all the violence and drug abuse that is present today, as well as promote good citizenship. For obvious reasons I believe that all of that can, and should be, the responsibility of the parents and the community-at-large, not by religious practices in the schools.

The other points I have seen that favor religion in our schools state that our country was founded by people who believed in freedom to practice one's religion openly and who used their religious beliefs to create the backbone of this nation. "*Our children should be able to participate openly in this great heritage, seeking help, strength, and endurance from God as did their forefathers.*" Again... WHICH GOD ARE WE TALKING ABOUT HERE? It is obvious that the Christian deity has been worshipped in this country for a long time, however in this multi-ethnic community of ours MANY religions are practiced.

Here is a 2000 U.S. Supreme court ruling that about says it all (Santa Fe v. Doe) "*School sponsorship of a religious message is impermissible because it sends the ancillary message to members of the audience who are non-adherents that they are outsiders, not full members of the political community, and an accompanying message to adherents that they are insiders, favored members of the political community.*" With reference to football games It goes further to state: "*The U.S. Supreme Court ruling today denying school sanctioned prayer at football games clarifies the intent of the First Amendment that such practices violate the separation of church and state. A public school sanctioned event such as a football game is not the proper forum for religion. This kind of sanctioned prayer intrudes on the rights of students who may feel compelled to participate or*".... I think you get the idea.

Theists do raise an interesting point, though, in one area. It seems to be common practice to employ congressional chaplains in our government.

We also have "*government recognition of holidays with religious significance such as Christmas or the proclamation of National Days of Prayer.*" I submit that this DOES happen, but there are a couple of reasoned, rational counter-points to make here, if I may. One obvious one is that 2,000 years of entrenched religion is a fact that we have to live with. We have all kinds of government buildings with references to the Judeo-Christian god. We have symbols, statues, and likenesses of Moses and many other biblical-related figures throughout our nation. All because of a man-made book.... Now THAT IS saying something about our community-at-large. My point, though, is to say that we have to start improving SOMEWHERE. There has to be a common-sense approach to all this. Normal people, NO MATTER HOW DEER-IN-THE-HEADLIGHTED they are about their respective religion, should NOT expect a public school to deliver a one-sided, one-religion aspect to the curriculum.

Religious-based holidays like Christmas. There are only 10 government-mandated holidays during the year, and Christmas and Thanksgiving are the only 2 remotely religious. I use the term 'remotely' because I think a great number of people nowadays see Christmas as a get-together and present-exchange, rather than a celebration of anything religious. I know that is only my opinion, but I am sure there are lots of folks who think in just the same way, and I hardly think that celebrating these holidays NOW justifies teaching religion in schools. We all know Christianity is in our history, and we expect old traditions like Christmas to continue. There is a big difference, however, between having fun once a year and subjugating kids to a religion they are not even ready for. THANKSGIVING was historically a religious observation to give thanks to God, relating to the Pilgrims surviving their winters. They had, evidently, a feast that consisted of fowl, venison, fish, lobster, clams, berries, fruit, pumpkin, and squash.... Well.... How do you suppose all of THAT got there? That's what the debates are all about, aren't they?

To be fair, the U.S. Constitution DOES allow and permit wide-ranging activities of a religious nature. It is ever changing, of course but here are some examples.

STUDENT PRAYERS

The gist of this is that the students can pray by themselves or with groups, as long as they are not disruptive. If they are in more informal settings, such as the school lunchroom or in the halls, a student may pray silently or audibly, but still be subject to the normal rules and regulations concerning regular speech. However, a line is still drawn to exclude 'preaching' to a group, or soliciting people for participation in prayer. Here is a ruling (from http://www.usconstitution.net) that is worth noting: "*In Good News Club v Milford Central School (533 US 98 [2001]), the Supreme Court ruled that a school may not exclude a religious club from using facilities in the school, after school hours, just because the club is religious in nature. In other words, if the Chess Club can use school property for after school meetings, the Good News Club must also be permitted to use school property. To deny them access is to discriminate on the basis of the Club's religious viewpoint, which is a violation of the Club's free speech. The point behind a policy to ban religious organizations in this way was to avoid Establishment Clause issues. But the Court found that it was clear that since the Club would meet after school hours, there was no way that it could be reasonably concluded that the school was endorsing religion.*" Fair enough..

GRADUATION CEREMONIES

There some benedictions, invocations and prayers at graduation ceremonies around the country, but most of these are in grey areas, as far as the courts are concerned. This is a hot topic amongst Christians and non-Christians alike, as they each vent their frustration over the current law excluding most religiously tinted graduation services. Christians are upset at the fact that their children should acknowledge their god as they are transitioning from being children to adults. Religious freedom is the concept here. Non-Christians object equally as strong as the diversity of our communities cries out for a more benign approach to religion. The practice of Christian values in schools (especially prayers) effectively discounts the deities of other religions as represented in a certain areas.

TEACHING RELIGION

While teaching a certain religion is NOT allowed in the United States school system, public schools can teach ABOUT religion. They can teach subjects like the history of religion, the role of religion in U.S. history and that of other countries' histories. All this can happen as long as no one religion is favored over another. From http://www.soundvision.com there are several other facts worth seeing. "*Students are allowed to express their beliefs about a religion in homework, artwork and other assignments. Teachers are required to evaluate this work based on academic standards.*" One that really surprises me, but is actually under the CLINTON DIRECTIVE is that "*Students can distribute religious literature to schoolmates. However, schools can impose restrictions on distributing this kind of literature as they do on other literature that is not school-related.*"

The basis for the Clinton Directive is briefly as follows. *"U.S. President Bill Clinton instructed Education Secretary Richard Riley to provide every school district in the United States with a statement of principles in 1995."* This statement discusses how far religious expression and activity are allowed in public schools. His directive also states that children are allowed "to wear religious messages on their clothing if they are allowed to wear comparable nonreligious messages."

There are many other areas, some in the 'grey-zone' and others that are universally accepted like the ones already mentioned, but it seems like a lot of the onus has been with the individual schools and their respective districts. One can only reasonably hope that they simply respect other peoples belief systems (or non-belief as the case may be).

Parents, try not to make your child a ward of the religion to which you happen to subscribe. Let them know about all religions and show how it is possible to have a great life (actually a better one from my point of view) WITHOUT religion. Then maybe the schools will follow.

Let us get on with the business of educating our children.

Chapter Fourteen

ATHEISM 101

A Primer

Now for some fun!

I thought I would have a chapter solely devoted to simple, basic arguments that the modern Atheist has when the 'big debate' is about to commence. I get most of these questions by way of researching many debates with Christopher Hitchens and Professor Richard Dawkins and others. Some I took from Atheist 'challenges' on the Internet. The responses are mine although probably similar to most atheist's positions, however most of these must be in your repertoire, should any of you have the opportunity to converse with a believer of any sort.

Theist comment first, then the atheist refutations (TH. - A.)

1) Ethical responsibility and morality issues

TH. "*Atheists cannot claim to have any objective moral base from which to draw. You make up the rules as you go along.*"

A. To say that we don't have an objective moral base may be true (the religious are hanging their hopes on this argument as religion was one of the first cohesive units for people to join, thus the 'GOD' figure would have been responsible for giving these folks their first 'objective' taste of what it was to be nice to people (?)) but that is missing the point. First, it is an assumption that one needs an objective standard to which one need to compare. I have already touched on the subject. Long before GOD came around people new that being nice and having solidarity amongst family and tribal groups led to more productivity and a better standard of living. Can you imagine living in a group of 100 people with everyone hating each other? You'd go mad. Not to mention that we may not have even made it as a species if this were true. We naturally know right from wrong. There are those among us who choose to disregard these 'normal' precepts of life, and most of them are in jail, so we do have a way of working things out by ourselves.

Vicarious redemption is another big one along these lines. It is basically Jesus dying for our sins past, present and future, and absolving all personal responsibility. This modern concept among the religious is still an important part of their belief, as amazing as it seems. A mostly immoral and primitive attitude, most well suited to the time the bible was being compiled, I am sure. I am also sure you have all heard the term 'scape-goating', the ancient practice of placing all the sins of a particular group on a goat and sending it away without food or drink, and left for dead. This would, as believed, wash away all the sins of that group. Personal responsibility must be a main component of our ethical and moral base otherwise we fail. The really bizarre thing is none of us asked for this. We were not present back then where Jesus was crucified, and yet we are (by religious doctrine) compelled to pray for redemption of our sins. Imagine, at the same time, that it is possible to be convicted of 'thought-crime', as Christopher Hitchens puts it, the best definition of a totalitarian regime. Condemned by something that we are thinking, plus the fact that we are not punished just when we are alive, but when we are dead as well! The New Testament has anyone that does not accept the message of god to be thrown into 'everlasting fire'.

If a theist asks you where you get your morality from, simply explain to them that in order for our species to have existed up until now we have had to draw from what I believe to be an innate ability to be reasonable towards one another. We NEED solidarity in order to survive. We needed it in the small tribes in our ancient past and we need them in today's modern world. No objective morality base needed.

1) Morality

TH. "*If there are no moral absolutes, or an objective moral base, how can you tell me that Pope Benedict XVI and Hitler are different in their thinking?*"

A. The fact that they ARE different (if any fair adjudication can be had) suggests that with or without an objective moral base, they act like they want to act. They each bring their own experience and personality to bear and make their decisions based on these. How can you tell me they are doing so BECAUSE of some objective moral teaching? Having laws today that say you have to spend 25 years in a federal jail for committing murder does not stop people murdering, so why would you assume that these two individuals NEED a moral absolute from which to draw? Hitler was a self-absorbed nut-job from the get-go and the Pope has his reasons for acting the way he does. Most of us can act just fine without the need to acknowledge an objective moral base. We CAN admit that religion has been with us for a while, but a lot of people acted perfectly fine before Christianity. From where, then, did THEY get their morals, huh?

2) Evolution

TH. "Why do you believe in evolution?"

A. For over 150 years the Theory of evolution by natural selection

(as well as other stimuli) has been tested and re-tested over and over and passed with flying colors. The brightest minds of our planet have been working on this for a long time. Science is the best way we have to come to any truth about our existence and how we grew to be who we are now. Certainly, there are always new ideas and new technology that have assisted in refining the theory, but the basics are fact. The evolutionary theory does NOT try to explain life's beginnings. It attempts to offer an elegant, scientifically reasoned way in which we all have grown from far simpler, less complex elements, and shows the amazing similarity between even the most remote of species. It offers a vast   fossil record with stunning intermediary fossils, showing a fairly linear progression of many species. One can see the major fossils at any decent museum.

To those theists that continue prodding and say that there are not enough fossils, 'show me the evidence', they say, reply that the fossils in the museums represent only a minute fraction of the fossils that scientists are studying, not to mention the DNA analysis and even more complex genome testing that is happening each day. Go to a museum and LOOK at the evidence, If that is not enough to convince you then you need to make arrangements to meet with an archaeologist and talk it over with him/her.

Another attack by theists is stating that there are "*not enough intermediary fossils to provide a linkage between a lineage*". You counter that whenever a scientist comes up with a fantastic intermediary, the theists question resounds even more blatantly. If you have two examples of a certain species and you find a possible linkage between them, you have found an intermediary. The theist will then exclaim that where there was only one gap now there are two. Sometimes you just can't win!

3) Life itself

TH. "What is your purpose of your life and what is the meaning of it?"

A. I often find this question most disturbing. I think (at least to me) that there are a lot of unhappy people out there who swear by their religion, and that is THEIR only purpose in life. Religion and worshipping a totalitarian commander gives their life meaning (?)

I, on the other hand, am always looking at amazing sunsets, being in awe of the huge expanse of the universe and watching pelicans ground-effecting their way over my local ocean close to the beach where I live. These are simple pleasures and afford me the chance to think and imagine what it was that allowed me to exist on this little planet in space. That's enough for me. I am a nice guy. I respect others. I enjoy sailing, golf, swimming, classic cars, electric conversions of gas-guzzlers (I'm on my first), writing books, writing music, and a bunch more. I enjoy life.

As far as purpose goes, I am here because I am the offspring of two parents, like most living things are. I have no intrinsic purpose other than to survive and be happy. The fact that I have self-awareness allows me to know that I enjoy certain things and can revel in them. Technically, my purpose here is the same as any other life form- to reproduce and survive to the best of my ability. The 'reproducing' concept has, so far, eluded me, however there is still time!

TH. "If in the end we all just die, and there is no immortality, what meaning do science, love, sculpture, writing etc. Have? It all seems to be for no reason at all."

A. I know that the idea of immortality sits well with theists. I also have shown that wishful thinking plays a big part in this idea, as I have seen no proof that someone can have an everlasting life (sounds like abject hell to me anyway). I really don't see the sequitur between life having meaning and living on immortally. Man is flesh-and-bone and has experiences here on earth as we all do. I hardly think one begets another. I enjoy life to it's fullest and then decompose. I enjoy life to fullest and then it's 'live on in an immortal condition?' What is the question you are REALLY trying to ask here?

4) Atheism is a religion and is fundamentalist in nature

TH "Aren't you just another religion, and fundamentalist to boot??" and "Why are you angry sometimes about the way religion operates?"

A. As explained earlier, atheism is not a religion. Simply tell the theist that your whole belief can be summed up as follows. 'There has been no evidence passed in my direction that would indicate that any god has existed, whether past, present or future.' There are no secret meetings, no churches, nor any 'holy book' to which we subscribe. We may get together, as the minority we are, to discuss our debates with theologians and present new ideas to each other, but that is about as far as it gets. If there are a small percentage of atheists out there giving us a bad name, simply ignore them.

As far as the fundamentalist issue goes, here is the obvious rebuttal. Fundamentalism is usually described as beliefs in a strict set of doctrines that perhaps fly in the face of reason and are unalterable beliefs. Atheism is the exact opposite. Atheists entertain the fact that we do not know everything and we welcome evidence as it crosses our path. With this evidence we come to our own conclusions using reason and critical-thinking, NOT WISHFUL

THINKING. Wishful thinking is the crutch of every theist who wants to brush aside any personal connection to responsible thought. Wouldn't it be nice if? Nice if our sins were washed away in the tide. Nice if we were given perpetual life in heaven. Please..... now I am tearing up.

5) Why we are atheists?

TH. "Why are you an atheist?"

A. In general, none of us would be atheists if there were no theism to be atheistic about! The relative close-mindedness and cult-like format of religion does make me rebel against the notion of anything religious. The fact that all religions are man-made and people still expect a huge amount of respect for their belief is another reason I am an atheist. The idea that you can be condemned for what you are thinking is another reason. Being told what to eat and on what day and who your sexual partner can be, are a couple more. Being told you will be in hell-fire damnation for a multitude of sins would be another. The fact that there are many different religions in the world and that they can't ALL be true (therefore none of them are) is another point in my decision in becoming an atheist.

This last point above is actually a big one, and I have yet to hear a confident theistic rebuttal of the question that states "If you are born of Indian parents, you most likely would be worshipping the Hindu gods. If you were born in Iraq I dare say you would be Muslim. If you were born to Anglo Americans, chances are you would become part of a Christian sect. Does it not therefore follow that, depending on where you were born, you would follow the stories and traditions of THAT religion??" THESE and a lot more made me 'become' an atheist. Like I have said, we are all born atheists. We need to be told about the weird stuff to become theistic.

We are in the modern world now. We can explain all the hurricanes and volcanoes and drought and famine and pestilence. We know what causes these things. We no longer need to sacrifice our first-born in the hope that we will get a better harvest next year, 'praise god'. These things and more are why I am an atheist.

Humorous break

TH. "What would you say to god if, when you died, you actually met up with him and could ask him a question?"

A. First off, I don't believe there is a god. For entertainments sake I think my first question might be: "Why did you wait so long to come to the aid of the people when we had been around for 100,000 years or more before you showed up and when you DID, you decided to introduce yourself through copper-age, illiterate Middle-east where your word spread as fast as molasses on a cold day?" My second question would be: "Why would you allow so much suffering on our world. Children being born with terrible diseases through no fault of their own and more. You can't tell me you were simply 'testing them'?

6) Dangerous religions

TH. "What is the most destructive religion today and in the past?"

A. ANY religion has the potential to wind in that small percentage of young people who have the potential to commit harm to others in the NAME of that religion. By their very nature, most religions offer a way to that 'perfect' place, in exchange for a few deeds, with usually catastrophic results. It is argued that Christianity poses no such threat, but a little investigation into it's past shows differently.

Any theist worth his/her salt would inevitably proffer the comment that none of the terrible deeds in the old and New Testament are carried out today. Nobody stones to death anyone for believing in another god. (No, but teaching of vicarious redemption still exists and is one of the major precepts of that religion). No one sacrifices an animal or person to appease his or her god. Fighting still goes on around religious lines, though. Ireland, Bosnia, Israel and Palestine. OH!! WE are back in THAT region of the world again! Tee-he- could not resist.

We, as a secular community, have seen that these behaviors are despicable and so no longer are they carried out. We have grown as a people, DESPITE the still-ancient teachings of today's biblical classes. Fundamentalist Christians and a whole bunch of evangelicals still believe most of the literal bible though. THAT, my friends, is a scary concept.

7) Changing your mind

TH. "What would it take to believe in a god?"

A. I would think that answer would be plain to anyone who has read this book so far. EVIDENCE. Pure and simple. No Philosophy. No metaphysical mumbo-jumbo. No wishful thinking. No allegory. Evidence. Then let me make my mind up in a reasoned, intelligent manner to come to a conclusion, one way or the other.

8) Religion, destructive or not?

TH. "Do you think the earth would be better off without religion?"

A. A lot has been discussed about the bad parts of religion and it's effect on people, both young and old. Religion has been said to be an evolutionary necessity for our species. It gave us comfort from the many

154

things we did not understand as a relatively primitive species. We were a scared lot. We were afraid of our very shadows. There was a relative comfort in searching for something outside of yourself and being part of a group. The bible was our first attempt at philosophy, literature, science and more, and it was indeed, a primitive man's attempt. As it was the ONLY way for the power elite to wield something over the heads of the masses, it is easy to see how it has been kept alive all these centuries. Scared into it, being indoctrinated into it from birth, and following it under threat of being hurt or worse, religion has survived to this day. Literal proponents of the bible still exist, and in significant numbers.

Do I think the world would be better off without religion? That is a difficult question. I almost feel as if I would be asking the majority of our people to go 'cold-turkey', with most unpleasant results. 'Too big to fail'? Maybe. If religion the world-over had NOT appeared when it did, perhaps we would be further ahead in all aspects of our culture. Perhaps the industrial revolution would have occurred a lot sooner? We would have, no doubt, divided ourselves along some OTHER lines (as, I suppose, we are hard-wired to do) but we certainly could not have done much worse, at least as far as warring with other nations and committing genocide are concerned. I think the emancipation of women would have occurred sooner than it had. I think slavery would have been abolished a long time ago. These things surely are debatable and are only my opinion.

9) TIME TRAVEL

TH. This question I have heard many times. "If you could kill all the despots of the past 100 years (POL POT, Stalin, Hitler) would I do it if time travel was possible?"

A. Well, I have covered what I believe about time travel, but if the axiom is to be addressed I would say this: Maniacs and despots would always appear, somewhere, no matter if there were religion on our planet or not.

This theist's question often is the result of an atheist showing how there is a natural progression from religious indoctrination to committing horrible deeds. They usually bring up the above trio of self-absorbed lunatics and pass them off as having committed these deeds in the name of atheism. Nothing, as we have already learned, is further from the truth. You cannot be indoctrinated into atheism. You simply have the evidence to assist you in determining if there are gods or you don't. What part of that leads you to blowing up yourself and others? Besides, two of the three were NOT atheists and LENIN WAS (yet you hardly ever hear about him in this argument). Stalin was a puppet of Lenin. Stalin wiped out ANYONE who was against the state. Religious folks just happened to be some of the ones who opposed the state. They were doomed-for. No, I would not have killed them back in time. Other groups would have surfaced. One picks ones fights and deals with them as they come.

10) ABORTION ISSUES

TH. "Do you think abortion is 'evil'?"

A. This is a strange question, but I understand the motives behind it. Most Christians believe that aborting an unborn fetus is killing a person, and are against it. Stem-cell research is also a no-no for the religious majority, as the best stem cells to use are, evidently, ones that come from the fetus, if I have my facts correct.

I realize this next comment is not going to go down so well, but here goes. People have been killing other animal species for food, sport, and entertainment since we came into being as Homo Sapiens. We have raped the planet of trees, polluted its atmosphere and wiped out important marine populations. We spill poisoned oil into our oceans and kill other people for land, women, resources, and because of different religious affiliations. NOW we are worried about aborting something that is a mere BEGINNING of a life form?? Get real! Many women abort because of medical complications. Some are drug addicts and don't want their baby brought into this world with their illness. Some are pre-diagnosed with awful diseases, or conditions that would greatly limit their enjoyment of life as most of us know it. I think there are MANY reasons why, with advice from other people, a woman should be allowed to terminate her pregnancy, okay.. Kill her unborn child.

'EVIL' is not something 'other-worldly' or relegated to the inhabitants of the invented hell. Evil is practiced every day by a small percentage of our species. We just have to accept that as fact. We deal with it the best way we can. Evil is seen in religious groups, while pretending to be shining examples of upstanding behavior, condemning real women in need of aborting their unborn children. I would venture to say that MOST abortions can be justified, and to force a woman to carry to term a child that is not wanted, too sick to function, or from the result of rape (and more) is real evil personified.

11) The animal Kingdom

TH. "Should we save other species from extinction?"

A. I wasn't too sure how this question was relevant to our overall discussion, but I warmed up to it. I did so only to reinforce the idea that over 99 percent of the earth's species have already gone the way of the dodo-bird. I DO think it is right to prevent extinction as a result of man's intervention in these animals ⸁ natural habitats. It is man after all, that reduces the numbers of these species. WE clear-cut forests and force animals into situations that they are unprepared for and lessening their living areas resulting in a diminishing food supply. Funny thing is, with our technological improvements in medicine, we have probably halted, or greatly slowed down, our own evolution. It will take a lot for us to be totally wiped out, but the approaching Andromeda galaxy will do a pretty good job, I suspect!

12) Other-worldly

TH. " Do you believe in ghosts, the after-life, aliens, or any other super-natural phenomena?"

A. "No." I mean, any theist questioning people's beliefs in other 'phenomena' that cannot be proven or explained is just in denial. Belief in a god, any god, is just as un-provable and as inexplicable as the next phenomena.

13) Special privileges

TH. Comment--"I am Muslim and I am greatly offended at that depiction of Allah in that cartoon and those few words in the music behind a video game.

A. We have all heard the reaction by vocal proponents of the Muslim religion, expressing anger at recent depictions of Allah in a cartoon, and several words in the background music of a video game. They say they are deeply offended as Allah is their 'rock' and source of their faith and that anything depicting their faith in anything but a respectful light is intolerable.

They seemed to be unmoved when the obvious response is given. I would say to the Muslim that their religion should be no more off limits to the same ridicule, characterization or humor that the rest of us have to deal with. What makes you so special? Religion is so entrenched in our society that it is seen as a way of life to a lot of folks. They assume that because they are a part of a 2,000 year-old religion that they have a built-in shield against any attacks. The fact that they are basing their entire lives on a man-made book is astounding to me. They are so blinded by their man-made religion that they cannot think clearly. ANYONE will tell you that a self-effacing attitude and an ability to laugh at oneself are great character traits to possess. How can anyone be so deeply involved in these cobbled-together religions that they throw all reason out the door and assume some kind of 'beyond reproach' posture? Simply unreasonable.

14) SYNCHRONICITY

The subject of synchronicity sometimes comes about when a person claims to have been an atheist for a certain period of time in his life, but then begins to experience two or more meaningful events that happen around the same time, but whose individual causation is different. Many combine this with suggesting that atheists look into themselves and become more spiritual, foregoing organized religion over milder forms of religious practice. Most people with an ounce of reason would call these synchronous events as coincidences. Carl Jung has written books on this subject, that he created, and is far too complex to get into here. It is, however, just another way so-called 'rational' people can convince themselves something is 'out there' but being inexplicable at the same time. WE have relatively finite experiences here on earth. We live in small communities and also areas of large populations. BOTH these societal living conditions pre-supposes that at some time one would ultimately experience a coincidental occurrence or two in ones lifetime.

There is no argument against this. If the person above were a true atheist, he would rationally dismiss these experiences as coincidences and move on, because that's all they are.

Here are some questions for atheists by 'Stewart the Man' in "Religion, June 18, 2009." They are sophomoric at best, but worth the entertainment value. These are supposed to be serious questions to which an atheist cannot have a decent answer.

Here are his questions and my basic answers:

+ "*Why are we here on earth?*"

We evolved from extremely minute forms of life as soon as earth was able to be in a state where this was possible. There are many documentaries and books on this subject. It took a long time, but we evolved the same way as every other species: through natural selection, speciation, genetic drift and a host of other processes. Millions of species have died out along the way to 'allow' us to be where we are. One change one-way-or-the-other and we would be totally different than the way we are. Or non-existent.

+ "*If intelligent design and the Bible aren't correct, then how did humans end up being the masters of every other species on Earth? Why didn't bears or deer develop intelligence and the ability to speak in thousands of different languages and the ability to build solid structures and the ability to civilize and the ability to master any environmental challenge?*"

Hmm... Why can't a bear talk? Probably because the 'branch' of the 'evolutionary tree' he was on did not pre-dispose his ancestors to develop the ability to create words, just grunts and frightening sounds (that's why I stay away from bears). Humans did not learn to speak intelligibly for a very long time. We grunted too. We developed at the end of the 'evolutionary tree' as we know it, so we have had a HUGE amount of time compared to other species to develop what we now have. It's rather silly to suggest that other animals should have had the ability to be us. It's not arguable. You might as well ask why we are not able to soar above our world like the golden eagle, or swim as deftly as the bottle-nosed dolphin! Next question please.

+ *"If the universe was entirely empty space except for a small mass of matter that created the universe by spontaneously exploding and steadily expanding throughout empty space. What caused that small mass of matter to explode?"*

If you care to do any research into this area it would enable you to have more of an understanding of what it is you are attempting to say. Firstly, there are quite a few theories of what happened. Some say it was not an explosion at all but a gradual expansion (much like a small balloon becoming a larger balloon). We see that expansion now. Some say that absolutely nothing existed before this 'singularity' and that space actually existed within that state. Scientists are looking at black holes and believe similar 'singularities' reside within each one. I am not a scientist and have no room to go into detail here. Please just read a few books on the subject and you will find some very intriguing possibilities, NONE of which postulate a supernatural being waving his magic wand to create the heavens and the earth in 7 days. Personally, I think he should have spent a bit longer at it. Maybe he could have given us a 'paradise moon' to go to for relaxation or something.

+ *"Have you ever seen the beauty of a newborn child in his/her mother's arms? In that moment did you not experience the feeling that 'my gosh, there really is a God?'"*

Yes. And No. Back in copper-age Middle East where the bible had its start, sure, I would have attributed the birth of a child as some sort of miracle. I may also have sacrificed that child in the name of god to appease him in some way. Those must have been truly barbaric times. I'm glad we have seen the light, and also know that every life-form on earth gives birth. Using one of your metaphors, the mother squirrel gives birth to her young as well. Do THEY need to worship or believe in a super-natural being too? I think they are happy just being squirrels and doing what it is that squirrels do, don't you??

+ *"If God was created by mankind as an explanation for life and the events that make it up and mankind is by nature evil, as Rousseau said, why didn't mankind worship themselves or a power of evil?"*

Well, why would you want to take Rousseau's account of things and take it as 'gospel'? Does not your very argument/question rely on a truth? Who says man is evil by nature, besides Rousseau? The BIBLE? Well then, you must be correct. If man was inherently evil then, I suggest, we would not be here to discuss it. If evil is supposed to be our base evolutionary contribution to our species, then we surely would have perished when we numbered only a few thousand on this planet.

Evolution has a way of working things out. We have advantages over other would-be predators and we have survived (it took a while). Man has a choice when confronted by an opponent. It suits both parties to act

162

unselfishly if there is to be a civil outcome for both parties. That is inherent in our nature. Sure, we need a little guidance by our parents and our society so we can keep the really bad guys inline. It works, more-or-less. Since man does NOT worship a power of evil are you intending that man DID NOT CREATE GOD? I take it you did not take logic classes in school. Also, if you care to see how barbaric the Old Testament was maybe it could be said that 'we' DO worship a god of evil, after all it has only been man's improvement as a being over time that has mellowed him out. God didn't make us improve. We did that by ourselves. If it was up to him, we'd still be offering up our first-born to appease him in some way.

+ "If God was invented by humans, then why do so many Biblical stories involve his punishment of humans that went astray? Wouldn't humans rather create a God that allows them to get away with whatever they want?"

I'm actually glad you posed that question. It speaks to the major reason man created God and the bible in the first place. As I mentioned earlier, the bible was man's first attempt at trying to figure out who he was, why he was here. It was our first attempt at philosophy, of science, and of writing a complete book of ideas. As time advanced it was also realized that the bible was a method of control and that is why Christianity is so widely spread-out today. Do you think that 99% of South America is Catholic by accident? No. It was shoved down their throats. It would serve no purpose to make a god that allowed people to do what they wanted. How could the writers of the bible control the masses that way? I suspect the people of ancient Middle East were doing reasonably well BEFORE the invention of the bible. They had nomadic tribes and large, loving families. The bible ruined everything. The people were powerless against it because of their relative ignorance and subjectivity to anyone or anything that had power over them. The bible sounded pretty authoritative, so they went for it. Alas.

+ "You say God doesn't exist. Why does each person have a conscious then? Why does every person have a knowledge deep within them of right and wrong?"

Let's start with the first one. The mind has well been studied for hundreds of years. We (scientists in the field and doctors) know exactly how the brain functions and can easily explain one's 'consciousness'. I do not need to explain it to you (even if I could), as there are rooms full of books to show how the conscious mind works. There is no mystery there. There certainly WAS back when the bible was being compiled, and the obvious primitive statements in the bible bear that out.

Finally a theist admits that ('deep within them', as you call it) we DO know right from wrong! Thanks a lot. I'm glad we agree on SOMETHING! We are self-aware; we do have an innate ability to create solidarity between us. We don't need a theistic god to be telling us what to do everyday. No other creature on earth needs it, why do you say we need it?

+ "What happens to us after we die? (I don't mean our physical body, I know that decomposes back to the dust (another phrase out of the Bible) but I mean to who the person is)"

I don't think I understood the grammar, but perhaps you mean what happens to the persons 'soul'? As I have said before, a person has no soul. The body dies with all it's component parts intact and decomposes like you say, like 100 percent of the other species on earth do. Sorry, that's all she wrote. Man's ability to be self-aware, to calculate, to think, to enjoy is all part

164

of being human. When we die all of that goes with each one of us. Dolphins are partially self-aware as well. Do the research. Do you think THEIR 'souls' survive after they die? Come on.

Here are some questions from a Jewish Philosopher. Part of his subtitle for his essay is 'Ten Questions No Atheist Can Answer Convincingly'. The author is Jacob Stein and the web page in which his questions reside is http://jewishphilosopher.blogspot.com/2006/07/questions-for-atheists.html. (You may have to click on 'Jewish philosopher' if the page 'is not found')

+#1 - If no supernatural Creator exists, how did the universe originate?

Jewish answer: *God created the universe.*

Well, no argument there, hahaha. No one knows how the universe started, my poor misinformed friend. You don't know, I don't know. Scientists are trying to figure it out. Your ancient texts written by man tell you otherwise? Then so be it. Knowing how the cosmos started back then is impressive, indeed. However, I wonder why Bronze-age man never made it to the moon or prevented cancer from happening? I suppose even THEIR science had it's limits, huh?

#2 - If no supernatural universal Designer exists, why is the universe suitable for the existence of life?

Jewish answer: *God deliberately designed the universe to be suitable for life.*

Man, you just don't quit. The universe (earth, I assume you are talking about, specifically, as I am not currently aware of any other existing planet that has been proven to be capable of sustaining life) has evolved over billions of years, as the rest of the universe has. No doubt there are other planets similar to ours in constitution, which allow some forms of life to exist. Read a biology text. Read works that really give you an insight into what it takes for life to form on this planet. My main thrust here is to get you to realize that just throwing your hands up and stating that 'God deliberately designed the universe to be suitable for life' is pure wishful thinking and contingent for you carry on believing what you do.

#3 - If no supernatural universal Designer exists, how did life originate?

Jewish answer: *God created life.*

"OBJECTION your honor, assumes facts not in evidence." One can't simply SAY that god created life, no matter how fervently you buy into this Jewish faith of yours. WE don't know exactly how life started but scientists get closer every day. Where is your evidence? Oh, by the way, your man-made holy book is not any kind of evidence. I, too, could write a book telling of all the wonderful elephants I saw flying over the Rockies last year.. Would you believe it? Why not? Just because you would think you would be alone in agreeing with me? NO 'safety-in-numbers' reassurance? No 'House of the Flying Elephant' in which to pray? SEE? It's all man-made stories you are buying into. You don't need them. Make your life less complicated and simply LIVE!!!

#4 - If no supernatural universal Designer exists, what caused the repeated disappearance of more primitive forms of life and the appearance of new more advanced forms of life?

(For example, at the beginning of the Mesozoic and Cenozoic.)

Jewish answer: *God created and destroyed several previous worlds before the current one.*

Where exactly are you getting these facts, the Bible? Millions of hours of research by scientists will reveal to you what probably happened to 99 percent of all species on earth that have since become extinct. There was no god. Why would he waste his time doing all that?? If he wanted us here, he surely could, in his infinite power, create us with a wave of his hand. Why bother creating amazing dinosaurs and then wiping them out after 500 million years of existence?? IT MAKES NO SENSE! You couldn't say god was 'testing us'. WE WEREN'T AROUND YET!

#5 - If we have no soul, why do we feel conscious of ourselves?

Jewish answer: *We have a soul.*

Please see one of the answers above.

#6 "If no covenant exists between God and the Jews, stipulating that the Jews must observe the Torah or be killed, why did the Germans kill 6 million Jews?"

Jewish answer: *The Jews made such an agreement with God as recorded in Leviticus 26. When European Jews ceased observing the Torah, they broke the agreement and suffered the consequences.*

Now, THIS one is a sad testament to how far religious faith and belief gets. I was having a bit of fun with these basic, elementary school level questions and the corresponding 'JEWISH ANSWERS', but this one takes the cake.

Are you saying, sir (with all due respect), that the 6 million Jews who suffered death at the hands of a military headed by a sociopath, actually died because they no longer observed the TORAH?? Is that what you are being taught? That disgusts me, sir. That ALONE should be enough to convince any sane, intelligent person on this earth that biblical teachings and religion should be stopped. Pure-and-simple.

CHAPTER Fifteen

Still much to be discovered

How does one end a book such as this? Have we learned anything new here?

Summing up, I would have to say that I think there is a great hypocrisy amongst the people of the world, especially (I might add) in the United States, as far as religion goes. We are a nation where around 80 percent of us believe in some sort of God, and yet, hearing comments on the major news networks and radio, you would think that we are simply a secular nation. Religion somehow commands a greater amount of respect than in any other area of our lives. Religion is swept under the rug and is barely mentioned on television or on the radio, unless there is some war involving different religious factions (aren't they all?) or suicide bombings, or maybe a debate involving Christopher Hitchens or Professor Richard Dawkins. Most Politicians are careful not to invoke the 'almighty', as doing so may have serious social and political consequences. We say that there is a definite separation of church and state and yet verbal blunders as recent as the now-infamous one by former president Bush, Sr. (As presented earlier in this book) shows that we still have a lot more work to do. There are hundreds of thousands of fundamentalist Christians quietly spewing their ravings to anyone who will listen. There are tens of millions more that believe that the earth is only 10,000 years old!!! HOW ARE WE GOING TO CHANGE ALL THIS?

Through education; by shaking off the superstitions of old and facing life's trials and tribulations head-on; by actually thinking.

We are not born theists. We are born, in a sense, atheists. One has to be TOLD to believe in a certain god, then, when enough people believe, the atheist can tell his/her story.....

A quick look at several websites on the supernatural, ghosts and astrology gave me some alarming statistics. They seemed to point out that a decent percentage of people believed in all three. By 'decent' I mean in the 20-70 percent range, depending on the category! Some scientists are studying the way the mind works and finds a complete connection from ghosts to religious belief. The only difference is that religion seems to be a benchmark for studying these other 'fringe' beliefs as religious belief is said to be a nearly 'human universal.'

As a theist there are questions you can ask yourself now, if you like. If you can try to answer them with some objectivity then you have moved up a rung or two on the 'enlightenment-ladder'.

Why do you pray every day? Why do you bow down and recite ancient texts to try to appease your gods? Why is it that you attend church every Sunday to listen to the pastor or rabbi (or what-have-you) talking about subjects that use quotes from primitive holy books? Why do you try to absolve yourself from wrong-doing and sin by invoking the memory of a supposed Jesus that died for all your sins, past, present and future? Why do you allow your infant children to pray before going to bed? Do you ever think to yourself " If I was born to Indian parents I would be worshipping a Hindu god and not the Judeo-Christian one?" Try to answer these questions honestly and see what you end up with.

Everything else in life one approaches with reason, experience, a certain amount of critical thought and a modicum of common sense. Do you get in your car and simply trounce on the gas pedal and fly wildly all over the place? No. You may have children in the back seat and you look both ways before entering an intersection and you watch your speed and you notice how much gas you have in order to get to your next destination. When you approach a hot stove and the phone rings, what do you do? I trust that you don't casually lean on the active, hot element while chatting on the telephone? NO, of course you don't. Why is it, then, when you have this theistic belief system (that in many cases runs your whole life), do you simply follow the herd and do what others are doing? What a colossal waste of your time and intellect! Think of all the other more constructive things that you could be doing with your life. At this late stage of this book I would say that if your response to this question was that you do it because your parents did it and that it was traditional and cultural and that you still are pretty certain that a god DOES exist somewhere, then all I can say is that I've tried and it's time to move on.

I think I have made my position clear throughout this book. If someone really needs to contemplate an imaginary being, shall we say, 'outside' of the natural self (and it brings them some sort of comfort or support) then I certainly do not want to deny any of my fellow earth-dwellers this opportunity. What doesn't work for some works for others.

I think I have given all of you a decent grounding in what I have learned, at least, as far as this big debate topic is concerned. As I claimed from the beginning, mine is neither an intellectual NOR a scientific approach to the content presented herein. Rather, I have condensed the major topics, shown a bit of the living fossil record, displayed some theists amazing ability to deny hard-and-fast facts on evolution, and more. I hope that some of you (all of you would indeed be 'wishful thinking') have enjoyed this little ride with me and that some of what I have presented has sparked the interest within you to convince others around you to adopt a more reasoned approach to these topics.

The actual, undeniable proof of god's existence one-way-or-the-other, in my opinion, will never reach us and will continue to be debated. Sometimes it is cathartic just to confront people of diametrically opposing viewpoints, hash them out, and see where they take us. The reality is far more important, however, to write this off as just another intellectual exercise, as I think I have shown all of you that if there WERE an all-powerful, omnipotent God that did not need an external cause to exist, and had dominion over us, it would be a very different world indeed from the one in which we live.

'Thank goodness' we do NOT live in that world, and that most of us are here, for better or worse, trying to seek solidarity amongst our planetary co-habitants and attempting at least to open up the minds of the believers, setting them on a path towards critical-thought, reason, and common-sense as it relates to their respective belief-systems.

All we see, hear, touch and smell can be explained very well WITHOUT the need for a celestial dictator, and I believe we would, as a people, be better off if more of us thought along those lines.

I will pray for you all.....

Finally, In our quest for knowledge; of trying to understand how we came to be on our small planet and, indeed, how the planet came to be at all, I can only quote a brief line from Thomas Henry Huxley, an English Biologist, who seems to sum it up best:

"The known is finite, the unknown infinite; intellectually we stand on an islet in the midst of an illimitable ocean of inexplicability. Our business in every generation is to reclaim a little more land."

"Poetry......

Thank-you all, and I hope you had a good time reading this. Soon you will be able to enjoy my second published book that is a direct rebuttal of a rebuttal of Richard Dawkins' book, THE GOD DELUSION. Douglas Wilson is responsible for his THE DELUDED ATHEIST, and I take it upon myself to show how his well-meaning but misguided efforts to thwart reasoned arguments against Theism, fall flat.

Acknowledgments and Source Guide

Chapter 1

Pinker, Steven. "The Moral Instinct." http://www.nytimes.com. 13 January, 2008. Web.

Chapter 3

"On Atheist Extremism." http://www. saintgasoline.com. 24 May, 2009. Web.

"Pentecostal." http:// www.faithmarketingalliance.com/pentacostal. 17 April, 2010. Web

http://www.jocys.com/dictators/#JosephStalin. Web

Futrell, Mynga, PHD. "Religious World-view". http://www.teachingaboutreligion.org. 5 January, 2001.Web

Chapter 4

Miller, Jonathan. "Jonathan Miller's Rough History of disbelief." http://www.youtube.com. Web.

"Top 80 Best Short atheist Quotes." http://www.milkandcookies.com. 23 February, 2010. Web

"Famous quotes about god." http://www.god-defined.com. 23 February, 2010. Web

"Theological Perspectives." http://www.uua.org. 1 June, 2010. Web

Chapter 5

Kreeft, Peter & Tacelli, Ronald, Sr. "Twenty Arguments For The Existence

Of God."

 http://www.catholiceducation.org. 24 February, 2010. Web

Chapter 6

White, Mike. "Scientists who do not believe in the theory of evolution respond to those who believe."

http://www.associatedcontent.com. 3 March, 2010. Web

"Richard Dawkins interviews Wendy Wright" (parts one through 7)
http://www.youtube.com/watch?v=YFjoEgYORo

Chapter 7.

Trowbridge, Geoff "The Whole Bible" http://www.maplenet.net. October, 1996. Web.

Schniedewind, William M. "Origins of the written bible,"
http://www.pbs.org/wgbh/nova/bible/written.

"National research center on human evolution." Cenieh
Classroom,geochronology. http://www.cenieh.es/en_ucc. Web

The Bible, Psalms (90:4)

Chapter 8

Gauvin, Marshall J. "The Bible, A Dangerous Moral Guide." From
"Fundamentals of Free thought"; 1922

Peter Eckler Publishing Company, New York.
Http://www.edwardtbabinski.us. Web

The Judeo-Christian Bible. Various Psalms.

Chapter 9

Hamilton, Donald L. Book "The Mind of Mankind." chapter-"How god created the universe."

http://www.novan.com/creation. 24 July 2010. Web

http://www.philosophyonline.co.uk/pages/docs/proofs.doc. Web

Chapter 10

Gijsbers, Victor http://www.positiveatheism.org. 13 June, 2010. Web.

Wikipedia. "Anthropic Principle" http://www.en.wikipedia.org/wiki. Web.

Reed DL, Smith VS, Hammond SL, Rogers AR,and Clayton DH. "Genetic Analysis of lice Supports Direct contact between Modern and Archaic Humans" PloS Biology Vol. 2, No. 11, e340 doi:1371/ journal.pbio. 0020340.http://www.pda.physorg.com. 21

January, 2010. WebKazan, Casey. "The 'Great Attractor'. What is the Milky Way speeding towards at 14 Million M.P.H.?" http://www.dailygalaxy.com. 20 March, 2009. Web.

Chapter 12

Osborne, Mike "A Primer on Pre-suppositional apologetics." http://www.freesundayschoollessons.org.

http://www.faithfacts.org/search-for- truth/questions-of-christians/is-christianity-based-on-blind-faith. June, 2006. Web.

Chapter 13

The Paleontological Society. "Evolution." Accessed June, 2009. http://www.paleosoc.org. Web.

Truth in science "The fossil record" accessed June, 2009. http://www.truthinscience.org.uk. And

http://www.evolution.berkeley.edu/evolibrary/article. Web.

Chapter 14

Gee, Henry/ Howlett, Rory/ Campbell, Philip. Nature Magazine. "Evolution Gems".

http://www.nature.com/evolutiongems. January, 2009. Web.

Chapter 15

Robinson, B.A. "Religion and Prayer in U.S. Public Schools." http://www.religioustolerance.org. 27 April, 1995. Web

"Religious Freedom in Public Schools". http://www.soundvision.com/info/education/pubschool. Accessed 4th June, 2010. Web.

Religion News Service. 15 July, 1995. http://www.articles.latimes.com/1995-07-15/local/me-24031_1_religious-expression. Web

Chapter 16

Stein, Jacob. http://www.Jewishphilosopher.blogspot.com. Accessed 7 August, 2010. Web.

Britt, Robert Roy. "Americans Believe in God, Astrology and Ghosts." www.livescience.com. Web.

Don't Tell Your Momma You're an Atheist

www.ingramcontent.com/pod-product-compliance
Lightning Source LLC
Chambersburg PA
CBHW060925040426
42445CB00011B/799